TROTSKY'S ANALYSIS OF SOVIET
BUREAUCRATIZATION
A Critical Essay

FLINDERS POLITICS MONOGRAPHS

A Series of Monographs in Politics and Related Disciplines

Series Editor: Dr Hin Leng

The Flinders Politics Monographs consist of discrete studies of topics, themes and contemporary political issues which will be of interest to a wide audience in the Social Sciences.

The Series is edited in the Discipline of Politics of the Flinders University of South Australia. Authors proposing a manuscript for inclusion in the Series should *first* send a brief abstract to:

The Editor,
Flinders Politics Monographs,
Discipline of Politics,
Flinders University,
Bedford Park,
South Australia, 5042.

Trotsky's Analysis of Soviet Bureaucratization

DAVID W. LOVELL
Department of Government
Royal Military College
Duntroon

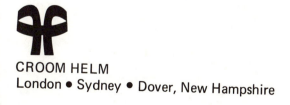

CROOM HELM
London • Sydney • Dover, New Hampshire

©1985 David W. Lovell
Croom Helm Ltd, Provident House, Burrell Row,
Beckenham, Kent BR3 1AT
Croom Helm Australia Pty Ltd, Suite 4, 6th Floor,
64-76 Kippax Street, Surry Hills, NSW 2010, Australia

British Library Cataloguing in Publication Data

Lovell, David W.
    Trotsky's analysis of Soviet bureaucratization.
    – (Flinders political monographs)
    1. Tro t'sk i, L.
    I. Title   II. Series
    320.5'32'0924   HX312,T75

    ISBN 0-7099-4112-9

Croom Helm, 51 Washington Street, Dover,
New Hampshire 03820, USA

Library of Congress Cataloging in Publication Data

Lovell, David W., 1956-   .
    Trotsky's analysis of Soviet bureaucratization.

    (Flinders politics monographs;)
    Bibliography: p. 76.
    Includes index.
    1. Trotsky, Leon, 1879-1940. 2. Communism – Soviet
Union – History – 20th century. 3. Soviet Union – Politics
and government – 1917-1936. 4. Bureaucracy – Soviet
Union – History – 20th century. I. Title. II. Series.
HX314.T73L68   1985   335.43'3   85-14968
ISBN 0-7099-4112-9 (pbk.)

Printed and bound in Great Britain by
Biddles Ltd, Guildford and King's Lynn

CONTENTS

PREFACE

It is not often that one has the opportunity to dust the years off an early essay, to rehearse and reassess half-forgotten arguments, and to present publicly what remains sound. I am grateful to the editors of the Flinders Monograph Series for encouraging me to review the work which forms the basis of this monograph, and to Norman Wintrop for his salutary influence on both versions. Of the central propositions of that early essay I am still convinced: that Trotsky's analysis of Soviet bureaucratization is inadequate to explain the character of the Soviet state under the rule of Stalin; that it does not substantiate his charge of 'degeneration'; and that it avoids the real issues posed by the existence of one-party states which profess a historic mission. I have, nevertheless, rewritten the work to give it a sharper focus as well as to incorporate a hypothesis about Trotsky's outlook which may admit further insight into his thought.

Since I first set down my views on Trotsky's analysis of the post-Lenin Soviet Union, a fine scholarly work on his social and political thought, written by Baruch Knei-Paz, has become available, and Trotsky has been promoted to the curious status of 'Modern Master' by Irving Howe and the publisher Fontana. Even a hagiography by Ronald Segal has appeared. Having already been generously, if tendentiously, served by the biographer Isaac Deutscher, and having recently had his autobiography (to the year 1929) published in a Penguin edition, the features of Trotsky's life and thought are widely known or easily ascertainable. I have therefore only sketched in material of wider theoretical or biographical significance. And because English-language editions of Trotsky's works are abundant, I have not presented a detailed investigation of the development of his views; intermediate stages can be explored by the diligent. Assuming that my readers have at least an elementary knowledge of Trotsky's politics and fate, I cannot but describe this work as an 'essay', although its length might tax even the patient.

Trotsky has not suffered the relative obscurity of some other Bolshevik leaders, such as the once-disgraced Bukharin and Zinoviev. Unlike them, he developed a coherent account of the Stalin regime and fostered groups of followers in Russia, at first, and then through-out the world. When not squabbling amongst themselves, these sects uphold the claims of their founder to enter the pantheon of social-ist revolution, in which only Marx, Engels and Lenin seem to have assured places. Yet they succeed only in perpetuating the myth of Trotsky's fall from revolutionary grace as a tragedy. They neglect the fact that on the need for Bolshevik Party rule, on the idea that polit-ical opposition to Bolshevism in power was hostile to the interests of the proletariat, and I suspect on much else that was fundamental to determining the character of the Soviet regime, Trotsky and Stalin were in agreement.

Why, then, does Trotsky continue to fascinate? As a theorist of socialist revolution in backward countries, he has been supplanted by Mao Zedong and Che Guevara. And as an architect and defender of the Soviet state, he is overshadowed by Lenin and Stalin. Rather, our attention is drawn to Trotsky the Oppositionist: proud, defiant and principled, who stubbornly struggled against the technique of the 'Big Lie', as Anton Ciliga called it, when so many others succumbed. For Leninists, however, principles are a luxury of opposition. Trotsky's sustaining concern was with the moral character of the revolutionary vanguard. To be a Bolshevik, for him, meant more than simply joining the Party: it was a position of responsibility, a title to be earned. The Soviet rulers, he believed, had drunk too deeply of the heady wine of power. Trotsky's puritanical code, given free reign during the hardships of war communism, caused friction between him and his Party colleagues, impaired his political judgement, and became a central element in his critique of Stalinism.

Trotsky used 'bureaucratization' to denote the moral degener-ation of the Party. Thus, despite his 'materialist' analysis of the Soviet regime, he complained that the revolution had been betrayed. Because Trotsky has helped to frame the subsequent debate about the USSR, it is important to determine whether his major contribu-tion is to the literature on bureaucratic rule, as is often held, or to the literature on revolutionary morality. I believe that moralism is a central ingredient in Trotsky's thought, and especially in his re-sponse to the outcome of the October Revolution. Other accounts minimize or neglect this aspect, or relegate it to his discussions of art and literature. In important respects, Trotsky reminds me of 'the In-corruptible' himself: Robespierre. Trotsky's Supreme Being was the socialist ideal; the October Revolution was his vocation. For him, Bolshevism was as much the moral outpost of socialism as it was the political vanguard of the proletariat.

The very spirit of the Republic is *vertu*.... The enemies of the Republic are the cowardly egoists, the ambitious and the corrupt. You have driven out the kings, but have you driven out those vices that their fatal domination bred within you?

 —Maximilien Robespierre

CITATIONS AND ABBREVIATIONS

The *Bibliography of Works Cited*, at the end of the text, indicates the editions used; page references are to these editions.

Note numbers in the text are enclosed in square brackets; notes will be found at the end of the text.

I have used the following abbreviations for works by Trotsky, or collections of his articles, frequently cited in the text:

CLO.... *The Challenge of the Left Opposition (1923-25)*, Pathfinder, NY, 1975.

RB..... *The Revolution Betrayed*, Pathfinder, NY, 1970.

IDM.... *In Defense of Marxism*, Pathfinder, NY, 1970.

TW..... *Writings of Leon Trotsky* (in twelve volumes), Pathfinder, NY, 1969–77.

In citations from *Writings of Leon Trotsky*, the abbreviation will be followed by a numeral to indicate the year to which that volume refers, then by a numeral to indicate the page number. Thus TW 1929,124 refers to page 124 of *Writings of Leon Trotsky 1929*.

All other citations in the text consist simply of the appropriate abbreviation followed by one set of Arabic numerals to indicate the page number.

I

INTRODUCTION

Trotsky arrived in revolutionary Petrograd in May 1917, a month after Lenin. At the Sixth Congress of the Bolshevik Party, in July-August 1917, Trotsky and his *Mezhraiontsy* group joined the Bolsheviks and Trotsky became a Central Committee member. As President of the Petrograd Soviet and Chairman of its Military Revolutionary Committee, Trotsky organized and led the insurrection which nominally placed power in the hands of the just-convened Second All-Russia Congress of Soviets of Workers' and Soldiers' Deputies on 25 October 1917 (old style). Trotsky soon became Commissar of Foreign Affairs in the Soviet government, and conducted the peace talks with Germany which culminated in the ignominious Treaty of Brest-Litovsk. Then, as Commissar of War, he commanded the Red Army to victory against the Whites and foreign interventionists. Although a 'new' Bolshevik, and despite his initial reluctance to adopt the term 'Bolshevik', [1] Trotsky quickly became a staunch Party man, identifying himself with the Old Bolsheviks, with whom he had often clashed. Perhaps he had finally accepted that a Leninist party made his theory of 'permanent revolution' complete, as Knei-Paz firmly argues it does. [2] Within twelve years of the Revolution, however, he had been expelled from the Party and exiled from the Soviet Union, protesting the policies and methods of the post-Lenin leadership.

The authoritarian results of the Revolution were not entirely unexpected. Even if we discount the consistent anarchist critique of Marx and the Marxists as malicious, and the criticisms by 'social imperialists' and other 'renegades' from the proletarian revolution, such as Karl Kautsky, there remain the forebodings of Rosa Luxemburg and even of some Bolsheviks, those whom Robert Daniels has called the 'conscience of the revolution'. [3] Trotsky never joined the ranks of those Bolsheviks who expressed unease about one-party rule. He was, however, the first Marxist with revolutionary and Leninist credentials (often challenged by those he criticized), to develop a coherent critique of the regime he helped to create, but which rejected him. Upholding the tenets of Leninism, he developed the idea of bureaucratization into a full-blown theory of a society trapped between

1

capitalism and socialism.

As a theorist, however, Trotsky was not what he seemed. Although he formulated the theory of 'permanent revolution', with some assistance from Parvus, and developed a Leninist critique of the Stalin regime, Trotsky had insights rather than theories. Unlike Marx, whose theories could not accommodate all his insights, Trotsky's insights were not quite enough to fill out and sustain his theories. Trotsky's analyses are often thoughtful, precise and devastating; but they contain unexamined assumptions which tend to close off lines of questioning. 'In our time' George Orwell wrote in the 1940s, 'it is broadly true that political writing is bad writing'. [4] And despite Trotsky's well-turned phrases, his vivid metaphors, and his ability to convince even able minds, Orwell's injunction applies just as much to Trotsky's work as it does to the hackneyed phrases that he himself cited. For Trotsky espoused, if stylishly, an otherwise unpalatable orthodoxy. Of course, Trotsky had considerable reserves of courage, and a flair for language and culture which briefly endeared him to many Western intellectuals, including Orwell. But his analysis of Soviet bureaucratization, in particular conceals or distorts an important and enduring dimension in his life and works: the moral dimension.

For Trotsky, public and private morality were barely distinguishable. With him, Mandeville's aphorism 'private vices, public benefits' found no favour. He demanded high standards of conduct from himself and from the Party he adopted—this attitude he came to call 'Bolshevism', and in some ways his construction of it downplayed important Leninist ingredients. '"The epoch of wars and revolutions"' he wrote in his final exile, 'is a harsh epoch. Pitilessly it uses up people—some physically, some morally' (TW 1929,373). His wife later spoke of 'the moral collapse of the old [Bolshevik] revolutionaries'. [5] Trotsky was prepared to use any means to attain socialism: to destroy other Soviet parties, to ban opposition within the Bolshevik Party and to ignore much of the best in the Western moral tradition. All this was done in order to preserve the Bolshevik Party in power. But how could he preserve Bolshevism in the Party? In the 1930s, defending the view that nothing was morally reprehensible which genuinely advanced the cause of socialism, Trotsky aimed to distinguish his moral outlook from the 'amoralism' of the Stalinists. As John Dewey, the American pragmatist philosopher, realized, [6] Trotsky did not properly answer the central issue of what means are appropriate to historical, long-range goals; in short, whether one generation should be sacrificed for the next. Rather, Trotsky's ar-

2

gument was a political one; it centred on the issue of what it was *genuinely* to advance the cause of socialism. [7] Crushing the soviet democracy at Kronstadt in 1921, for example, was in the interests of the Revolution; Stalin's purges were not. Yet Trotsky's appeal for *Soviet* government had convinced the Kronstadt sailors to join the Revolution; his defence of *Bolshevik* government drove them to rebel. [8] Although an instrumental view of morality informed all of Trotsky's work, and can be seen more as a means of justifying than guiding actions, there was also a positive, but unwritten code which he applied to the Party. Deviation from this code of revolutionary honour was deviation from Bolshevism itself.

Trotsky joined the Bolshevik Party at an extraordinary moment in its history. The Bolshevism which he championed for the rest of his life may have been too much influenced by the circumstances of 1917, when the Bolshevik Party under Lenin was the only consistent party of revolution. With Stalin at the helm, it succumbed to the temptations of power. Trotsky concluded that Bolshevism no longer existed in the Party. He took the spirit of revolutionary optimism and heroism as the spirit of Bolshevism. Lenin's organization and methods, once abhorrent to him, were subsumed under the Bolshevik commitment to revolution. Had it involved a change of personnel for careerism to become the dominant mood of Party members? Although much of the Central Committee of October 1917 was, twenty years later, dead or murdered by Stalin, that may not be so of the less vaunted Party leaders.

The subject of this inquiry, however, is Trotsky's analysis of Soviet bureaucratization, which is sometimes seen as one of the most cogent explanations of the Soviet phenomenon. Trotsky believed that Bolshevik moral standards declined after the Revolution because of the integration of Party and state, and because there was no force on the Party from above (such as the Lenin, or him), or from below (such as class conscious workers, who were killed or exhausted in the First World and Civil Wars) to keep the Party on its proletarian course. He did not, however, advocate Soviet democracy or the constitutional guarantees of liberties, which have acted in other states as brakes on the ambition and power of political leaders. Trotsky saw no inherent dangers in the existence of one-party states. In fact, in the early years of the Soviet regime he proclaimed that only the dictatorship of the Party made possible the dictatorship of the Soviets. [9] Yet in his Presidential address to the Petrograd Soviet in September 1917 he had liberally declared:

3

we shall conduct the work of the Petrograd Soviet in a spirit of lawfulness and of full freedom for all parties. The hand of the Presidium will never lend itself to the suppression of a minority. [10]

It is also clear that in 1917 Lenin was far less concerned about the 'democratic' or 'constitutional' niceties of insurrection than was Trotsky. Nevertheless, after taking power, other Soviet parties were progressively outlawed.

The elements of Trotsky's critique were not wholly original with him; concern about bureaucracy had a tradition in the Party, and was echoed by Lenin himself. I have examined Trotsky's analysis of bureaucratization, rather than of bureaucracy because there is little analysis of the latter. If we are to understand the structures and functions of bureaucracy we would do better to look at the established figures in this field, notably to Max Weber. Trotsky does not tell us much at all about the Soviet bureaucracy, even though he claimed to analyse it and its power. What he really objected to, as a close reading of his works reveals, was not bureaucracy as such, or the advance in its control over new areas, but bureaucratization. He used this term as a code for the debasement of the Bolshevik Party's moral fibre. Trotsky found evidence for a growth in the power of the bureaucracy in the prevailing manners and characteristics of Party members. It was certain reprehensible 'habits' and 'attitudes' which he took—not altogether fairly—as characterizing bureaucracy, that he believed had permeated the Party, and had led to the regime losing the confidence of its people.

Trotsky's analysis of Soviet bureaucratization has had its share of accounts and interpreters, many of which sympathetically hint at the contest between David and Goliath, although Lev Davidovitch did not come off quite as well as his biblical namesake. Biblical analogies were not foreign to Trotsky's work; he condemned Stalin as 'Cain' (TW 1937–38,270) and as 'Judas'. [11] Trotsky's *The Revolution Betrayed* is often held to be an invaluable analysis of the Soviet disease; a recent issue of the *New Left Review* lavishly described it as a 'masterpiece'.[12] But Trotsky was blinded by his own preconceptions, and there were certain things which—not by psychological predisposition, as some have supposed, but by theoretical commitment—he could not question. And is it really bureaucracy that Trotsky analyses, or a host of other but related issues under the one rubric: for example, the merging of Party and state, the 'bad manners' of Party secretaries?

When first confronted with bureaucracy, as a concept in Hegel's political philosophy, and as censor of the *Rheinische Zeitung*, Marx

4

tended to link it with the old regime, with German ways of doing things. He believed that the bourgeoisie—whose motto was cheap government—would do away with it. But 'bureaucracy' assumed a more important role in his 1852 *The Eighteenth Brumaire of Louis Bonaparte* as the social basis of the political success of Louis Bonaparte. Marxists generally agreed that under socialism the state would have been 'abolished' and that (in the Saint-Simonian phrase) 'the government of men would be replaced by the administration of things'—a distinction that they have yet to explain satisfactorily. Undeterred, socialists adopted this phraseology, even though they were not keen to specify their plans for the future society. In the Second International it came to be considered a virtue (especially in the face of hostile questioning) to have no blueprints for the future. Many critics, however, pointed presciently to the danger of a huge growth in the state, of citizens being oppressed by all-powerful state officials. They recognized that the market discriminates between people only on the size of their wallets; the socialist state discriminates against those who do not bow before it.

Trotsky was instrumental in the creation and the defence (both material and intellectual) of a one-party state. He accepted Lenin's overriding belief that the Bolshevik Party alone represented the historic interests of the proletariat. That 'representation' formed the crux of his commitment to the Soviet state, and was the basis for his pathetically ingenuous statement in 1924 that one could not be right against the Party: 'Comrades, none of us wants to be or can be right against the party. In the last analysis the party is always right' (CLO,161). But he would soon be hoist with his own petard, for he did not specify how the Party was representative—especially since he agreed with Lenin that the traditional means for determining such things (elections and the free play of opposition parties) were inherently 'bourgeois'. Trotsky claimed (at the time) that the Lenin Levy—a huge Party recruitment campaign ostensibly to honour the memory of Lenin, who died in January 1924—was a measure of proletarian confidence in the Party and confirmed that Bolshevik rule was democratic. It was, according to him, more valid evidence than the formal rules of parliamentarism (CLO,160).

Trotsky could not specify any institutional means to ensure that such representation was genuine and continued after Lenin's death. Instead, he concentrated on the 'moral' character of the leadership. His stress on the importance of leadership, especially during the 1917 Revolutions, is by now well known. But after the Bolshevik seizure of power he began to attend to its moral dimension, to the enormous

5

historical and other responsibilities of leaders *vis-à-vis* the masses and socialism. He emphasized this theme in his 1924 'Lessons of October', which attempted to embarrass Zinoviev and Kamenev by broadcasting their 'lack of nerve' in 1917, right down to the major programmatic document of his Fourth International:

The world political situation as a whole is chiefly characterised by a historical crisis of the leadership of the proletariat. [13]

What was the difference between the one-party dictatorship under Lenin, and that under Stalin? Since there had been no significant institutional change, Trotsky argued that the Party was not the same party which had taken power: bureaucratization had changed it.

The core of this essay consists of four chapters. Chapter 2, focusing on Trotsky's 1923 *New Course*, examines Trotsky's initial attempts to comprehend and remedy what he saw as dangerous defects in the Party. Lenin, too, had expressed fears about the fate of the regime after his demise. It has been noted that Trotsky cherished an ambitious conception of his place in history; [14] his defeat in the 'new course' campaign, he considered, was a turning-point in Soviet affairs. In 1929 he argued that there had been two major stages in the Soviet revolution: 'Lenin's illness and the opening of the struggle against "Trotskyism" can be taken, roughly, as the dividing line between them' (TW 1929,46). Unwilling to link these stages solely with his defeat, Trotsky nevertheless placed great store by the fortunes of individuals, later tempered by his desire to denigrate the role of Stalin:

the fight between individuals and groups in the USSR is inseparably bound up with the different stages of the October Revolution. (TW 1929,117)

The touchstone for his conclusion in 1933 about the death of Soviet Bolshevism, however, was his view that the rise of Hitler in Germany had been permitted by the policies of the German (and Soviet) communists. This conclusion is examined in Chapter 3. The next deals with the other major document in Trotsky's struggle against bureaucratism, *The Revolution Betrayed*; Chapter 5 with his defence of its central theses against a challenge from within the ranks of his own followers.

The possibility of new forms of oppression or exploitation arising in post-capitalist societies is a theme which has a tradition in the socialist movement predating even Michael Bakunin's critique of Marx. Accusations of authoritarian motives among the early socialists abounded. They also, of course, have their conservative counterparts. Among socialists, such theories usually centre on the idea of a 'new class', and the Marxists—particularly with their doctrine of the

6

dictatorship of the proletariat—have long been slow-moving targets of this kind of attack. As I have pointed out elsewhere, [15] the concept of the dictatorship of the proletariat is inadequately described by Marx, and the term itself seems a particularly unfortunate one for those Marxists committed to democracy and schooled in the Western liberal tradition; many of them have tried to ignore it. Lenin, however, brandished the dictatorship concept against his opponents in the Second International and in the Russian Social Democratic Labour Party, insisting that it was the essence of Marxism.

Trotsky's contribution suggests a new approach: a society foundering between capitalism and socialism, an indeterminate society. But when would the forms of Soviet life become stable; when could the jury of history to which he appealed bring in their verdict? Trotsky believed that the Second World War might provide the answer, but he did not live long enough to take the Soviet victory and subsequent territorial expansion into account. Trotskyists have since been vehement about this question of the 'nature' of the Soviet Union, which they see as one of Trotsky's major contributions to modern political analysis, and as the touchstone of revolutionary politics. In 1965, two American Trotskyists averred that

The attitude taken toward the Soviet Union throughout all these years has been the decisive criterion separating the genuine revolutionary tendency from all shades and degrees of waverers, backsliders and capitulators to the pressure of the bourgeois world. [16]

For them, the jury of history will always be out.

If Trotsky did not give rise to, he has at least provided a major impetus for, a genre of literature and political analysis which stresses the 'bureaucratization of the world'—to borrow the title of Bruno Rizzi's best known work, and the sentiment of James Burnham's *The Managerial Revolution*. But the 'bureaucratization thesis' is a response to the Soviet (and Nazi) phenomenon of this century from a political perspective which ignores questions that others see as crucial. It is a thesis that trades on the fact that as more demands are placed on the modern state, ever more powerful and complex bureaucracies arise. There is no doubt that bureaucracies have grown more extensive and powerful in all countries, and play a major role in statist economies. But in what sense can 'the bureaucracy'—if there is such a thing, and not simply many bureaucracies—'rule'? This is the question which is handled so poorly in the 'bureaucratization thesis', because of its reliance on Marxist categories—for the Marxists cannot agree on how classes rule, or what they mean by 'ruling'. In short, the 'bureaucratization thesis' does not substantially contribute

7

to our understanding of bureaucracy, even if it points to some of the dangers of bureaucracies. I shall explain below why this is so.

BOLSHEVISM BESIEGED

Trotsky's declaration of a Soviet government in October 1917 was an attempt not just to seize the propitious moment but to legitimize the Bolshevik coup in the name of the Soviets. It was a declaration of war upon the Provisional Government, with which the Soviets had coexisted uneasily almost since the February Revolution. 'Dual power' had meant that one government did not have the authority and the power to suppress the other, and therefore had, however reluctantly, to accept its existence. Trotsky gambled that the time was ripe for a decisive test of power. The declaration was not a democratic or legal act in any formal sense, although Trotsky would later make much of the idea that it was. It was a question, rather, of whose law would hold sway. The Bolsheviks thus precipitated the Civil War, whose ferocity and destructiveness indicate just how tenuous was their claim to popular support in 1917.

For Trotsky, as for Lenin, opposition parties—even socialist and Soviet opposition parties—were expressions of the interests of social forces ultimately hostile to the proletariat. On the basis that the Bolsheviks, and through them the state, actually represented the workers' interests, Trotsky urged toward the end of the Civil War the militarization of labour: the introduction of military organization and discipline into the workplace. Since the state represented the interests of the workers, he argued, they had no need of the protection afforded by trade unions. Lenin retorted that although in Russia there was a workers' state, it was a state with bureaucratic deformations. Lenin used this argument perhaps more in order to placate the leaders (and members) of trade unions, who formed an important material force supporting continued Bolshevik rule, than to dissect theoretically the Soviet state. There had earlier been strikes against certain Bolshevik decisions, and Lenin at least realized that brute force was not a sufficient base on which to rule. Lenin was here a consummate politician; it was this sense of politics that Trotsky never fully grasped. He was more interested in following the logic of the the matter. Trotsky's argument grew from the premise that the state and Party had become one—a notion which Lenin rejected. In fact, Trotsky soon began to claim that the Party had faltered because it was enmeshed in the Soviet state.

By 1920, the Party may have been militarily secure, but it still had to rule over—not simply to terrorize—a population which was largely peasant. It had conciliated this section during the Revolution by adopting almost unchanged the agrarian programme of the Socialist Revolutionaries, and had acquiesced in peasant expropriations of land. This policy, or deferral of policy, ensured that White armies during the Civil War found little support in the countryside. Afterwards, Bolshevik rule still depended on the peasant, just as their hopes for a revival of industry depended on good harvests and a lack of hoarding. Forced requisitioning had created tensions between the peasants and the Bolsheviks and, as the Bolsheviks realized during the period of the New Economic Policy, the decreasing prices of agricultural goods and the increasing prices of consumer goods meant that they had to tread warily. Decisively dealing with the peasants had to be postponed until the Bolsheviks were more firmly in power. The workers, too, were not entirely enamoured of Bolshevik rule. Their trade union organizations still had some measure of independence, and they were prepared to strike in protest at the more repressive Bolshevik orders. They, too, had to be coaxed.

The Bolshevik Party ruled by the consent of many of the people, but it could not do just as it pleased. It had yet to break up all social forces independent of it. The Party itself faced novel problems. It was larger than ever, and Trotsky soon began to question the motives of many of those who joined when its dominance had been secured. There were no precedents for policies to be followed, nor for how they should be determined. As long as Lenin was alive there existed within the Party a certain freedom of discussion, sometimes circumscribed in perilous situations, such as the Kronstadt rebellion.

The Party did not have a strong tradition of democracy. If Lenin could not get his way by force of better arguments, or his authority, and if he believed the issue was crucial, he resorted to ultimatums. In September 1917, he threatened to resign from the Central Committee over the question of the impending insurrection. [1] And in February 1918, he did the same over the question of peace with Germany. [2] Furthermore, during the early years of Soviet power there were shifting political alliances in the Central Committee, which hardened after Lenin's death. Trotskyists have always emphasized the closeness of Lenin and Trotsky, and particularly their 'alliance' on economic policy and the national question in the last stage of Lenin's life. Opponents have been keen, on the other hand, to insist on the differences,

10

particularly (but not only) before 1917. But Lenin's relations with Trotsky were not more fundamental than his relations with Stalin, or vice versa, nor was there a profounder closeness of principle between Lenin and Trotsky (or a profounder difference). This style of political argument does not take into account the fluid, tactical and temporary nature of post-Revolutionary Bolshevik leadership alliances. Trotsky, without the moderating influence of Lenin upon the other leaders, became isolated from them. Ironically, he came increasingly to see himself, in Lenin's absence, as the foremost representative and genuine embodiment of his recently adopted party. To stop Trotsky acquiring Lenin's mantle, Stalin made a pact with Kamenev and Zinoviev. Whether Trotsky was aware of the bloc formed to frustrate his ambitions (and in some accounts he seems very much an innocent abroad), he saw in the thwarting of his proposals a decline in the character of the Party.

On 8 October 1923, therefore, Trotsky opened his campaign to reform the regime, and revitalize the spirit of the Party. In a letter to the Central Committee he raised two issues, one procedural, the other on policy, which were to feature in the brewing storm: party democracy and industrialization. His efforts 'over the past year and a half', he explained, to influence the highest levels of the Party against the dangers of the current organizational trend and to reverse a mistaken economic policy having achieved little, he threatened to widen the dispute to other elements of the Party. This sort of threat was very Lenin-like, but it recoiled on Trotsky. For although he deferred only to Lenin among the Bolsheviks, and thought himself in some cases Lenin's equal, few Bolsheviks rated him as highly.

Nevertheless, Trotsky's dissatisfaction with, as he put it, the 'extraordinary deterioration of the situation within the Party since the Twelfth Congress' (CLO,51) soon found a chorus in the 'Declaration of the Forty-Six'. These were not rank-and-file Party members, but experienced revolutionaries; Trotsky's message had clearly gone beyond the sanctum of the Central Committee. The forty-six formed the basis of what would soon become known as the Left Opposition. Fearing that the Party might split, the Stalin-Zinoviev-Kamenev triumvirate responded by condemning the Opposition's 'factionalism'. The triumvirate also attempted to ward the blow by charging, as it had done earlier that year, [3] that Trotsky's motive was merely to succeed the gravely-ill Lenin.

The most serious of Trotsky's charges related to bureaucratization and the accompanying lack of Party democracy. He attacked the 'fundamentally improper and *unhealthy regime within the party*'

11

(CLO,52), as well as what he called 'secretarial bureaucratism'. General charges against the internal Party regime were not new, and the campaign against 'bureaucratism' had been going on for a year or more within the Party. Trotsky himself had prosecuted the case against the Workers' Opposition both at the Executive level of the Communist, or Third International and at the Eleventh Congress of the Bolshevik Party. At that congress, in 1922, 'he confronted the Opposition as mouthpiece of the Bolshevik Old Guard, demanding discipline, discipline, and once again discipline'.[4]

What had now changed? Why should Trotsky himself not be called to order? Although he still considered himself the genuine representative of Bolshevism, he now sought to protect it against a leadership which was deserting and a membership which was allowing it to. In the name of Bolshevism, Trotsky appealed to democracy, which he contrasted to the centralism which had served its function of preserving the Party in a hostile environment before the Revolution and in a dangerous situation during the Civil War. The beneficial effects of democracy, however, were not extended by Trotsky to the whole of the Soviet system. As he put it:

The Twelfth Congress of the party took place under the aegis of democracy.... It was absolutely clear that the tight hold that characterised the period of war communism should yield to a livelier and broader party responsibility. (CLO,55)

But by October 1923, Trotsky warned, another organizational trend had become apparent:

The *bureaucratisation of the party apparatus* has reached unheard-of proportions through the application of the methods of secretarial selection. (CLO,56)

Trotsky referred to the growth of the power of Party secretaries, who controlled appointments to all the divisions of Party and state. This secretarial hierarchy had concentrated decision-making into its own hands at the expense of Party members. It was to this hierarchy that Trotsky attributed the bureaucratism which became the central theme of his *New Course* articles, written at the end of 1923. In the practice of the Old Guard 'to think and to decide' for the Party, and in its basic distrust of the Party, Trotsky saw the expression of bureaucratism. Again and again he contrasted this attitude, this trend of bureaucratism, with Party democracy.

But what basis is there for thinking that the essence of Bolshevism consists in the democracy of the type which Trotsky seemed to be advocating: that is, the ability of members freely to express opinions diverging from the Party line, and to elect anyone they chose

12

to positions of Party responsibility? Oppositions of many types had been tolerated in the Bolshevik Party, but this tolerance was never formally recognized in its organizing principle, 'democratic centralism', and existed by and large only when the Party was confident in itself and its leader. When Lenin's health began to wane, so did that confidence.

Left Oppositionists wanted a reintroduction of the atmosphere of debate and discussion which they said had characterized the Party even during the Civil War. They wanted more initiative to come from the ranks. It was easy enough, Trotsky argued in a speech to the Party's Thirteenth Congress, to ensure unanimous votes for the leaders' decisions in Party cells, but not in a way which encouraged internal Party life (CLO,150). He would later call for the reintroduction of the secret ballot to prevent the intimidation of Party members. The Opposition advocated broader participation in all aspects of Party decision-making: from formulating policy, to its debate and adoption, and finally to its implementation. This was at the core of the proposed *new course.*

Trotsky's appeal to democracy, and to the traditions of the Party which he argued upheld democracy, had an ulterior purpose. This became clearer at the Thirteenth Party Congress:
We have experienced too much history, and in particular too great a struggle against political falsifications, against margarine democracy—which is Menshevik ideology on the one hand and on the other, imperialism's last screening device—to approach the question of democracy from a formal point of view. (CLO,152)
Trotsky always found margarine rather distasteful. Twelve years later, he cited the emergence of the margarine industry in the USSR as evidence of the consumption privileges of Soviet bureaucrats, who, he claimed, ate butter (RB,119). For him, democracy was not a question of the frequency of elections, or the formalities of parliamentarism: it was the outcome which mattered. He hoped that by introducing new blood to the debates and leadership that the sharp distinction between leaders and led—even within the Party—would be overcome, and that the policies of the Party would change. The leaders' isolation and increasing power, he believed, diverted them from their real responsibilities to the working class. Democracy, for Trotsky, was a means for correcting the policy course, for renewing the proletarian links and orientation of the Party. It had no independent or overriding value. Yet there had never been any established institutional or procedural means for ensuring the link between Party and proletariat.

In the face of these—still confidential—protests, the triumvirate decided upon a tactical retreat. On the sixth anniversary of the October Revolution (7 November 1923, new style), Zinoviev publicly endorsed the 'practical application' of party democracy, and newspapers were opened for public discussion of the issue. *Pravda's* circulation doubled. [5] The Opposition seemed to gain ground, but the Party apparatus retaliated by removing critics from their posts. The Central Committee of the Communist Youth (Comsomol) was 'replaced'. Ill-health—a crucial factor in a number of Trotsky's most important campaigns [6]—prevented Trotsky from actively participating in the debate. But his vote, which made the Politburo unanimous, reinforced the triumvirate's 'New Course' resolution, promulgated early in December 1923. Trotsky's supporters suspected that this resolution was merely a ploy, even though Trotsky's formal support for it undermined their own position.

On December 8, *Pravda* published Trotsky's letter to Party meetings, which attempted to clarify his position. While upholding the recently adopted 'New Course', Trotsky stressed that its success would depend on rank-and-file pressure on the bureaucrats. He publicly expressed doubts about the sincerity of the sponsors of the resolution:

Before the publication of the decision of the Central Committee on the 'New Course', the mere pointing out the need of modifying the internal party regime was regarded by bureaucratised apparatus functionaries as heresy, as factionalism, as an infraction of discipline. And now the bureaucrats are ready to 'take note' of the 'new course', that is, to nullify it bureaucratically. (CLO,126)

This letter became a signal for further Opposition agitation to ensure that the resolution was enforced. It soon led to a concerted offensive against them.

The attack was begun simultaneously by Stalin and Zinoviev on December 15 in the press and at Party meetings. Its target was 'Trotskyism'. *Pravda* published a series of articles by Bukharin at the end of the year, entitled 'Down with Factionalism'. It was, as E.H. Carr has written, the 'first systematic essay in that unashamed exploitation of Trotsky's past differences with Lenin which afterwards became a major feature of the campaign against him'.[7] Adding to this counter-attack, support for the Central Committee came from provincial and country Party meetings to which the discussion had recently been extended. Trotsky's illness becoming more acute, he left Moscow early in January to recuperate near the Black Sea. In his absence, the Central Committee's campaign acquired momentum. A Moscow provincial Party conference expressed confidence in the current leadership, although the Opposition disputed that it was representative of Party feeling. Oppositionists argued that they had been cheated of majority support in the Party's ranks by the very apparatus they opposed. [8]

At the Thirteenth Party Conference, held in 1924, only three of the one hundred and twenty eight voting delegates represented the Opposition. The Conference was carefully staged by the apparatus to rout the dissenters. The Opposition, the leadership claimed, was not only an attempt to revise Bolshevism, not only a direct departure from Leninism, but a plainly declared petty bourgeois deviation. [9]

This sort of 'class analysis' was a feature of Lenin's style. Before the October Revolution, Lenin consistently labelled his political opponents as class enemies. It was often a substitute for reasoned debate. After the Revolution, he was more careful with the epithets he used to describe oppositions within the Party, but warned:

Whoever brings about even the slightest weakening of the iron discipline of the party of the proletariat (especially during its dictatorship), is actually aiding the bourgeoisie against the proletariat. [10]

Lenin's version of class analysis was accepted by Trotsky, and by the other Bolsheviks; indeed, it seems that Trotsky thought of the triumvirate what they openly charged of him. But he had not the organizational means of making its opprobrium stick. Hardly had the battle been joined than Trotsky was outmanoeuvred.

Trotsky's *New Course* pamphlet, delayed in publication and limited in circulation, [11] did not have a major influence on debate at the Thirteenth Conference. Yet as Deutscher remarked, 'these articles contain in a nutshell most of the ideas which at once became the hallmark of Trotskyism'. [12] Trotsky's moralism, in particular, became evident. In relation to the previously ill-defined evil of bureaucratism, against which everyone could inveigh, his ideas were beginning to focus. In particular, the danger of bureaucratism was now seen as the degeneration of the Bolshevik Party. A great deal was thus at stake:

It is only by a constant active collaboration with the new generation, within the framework of democracy, that the Old Guard will preserve itself as a revolutionary factor. (CLO,125)

For Trotsky, bureaucratism meant the Party's increasing alienation from the masses, and the tendency for political leadership to give way to mere administration:

bureaucratisation threatens to detach the leaders from the masses; to bring them to concentrate their attention solely upon questions of administration, of appointments and transfers (CLO,72)

15

leadership takes on a purely organizational character and frequently degenerates into order-giving and meddling. (CLO,77)

He believed that the behaviour of the men of the apparatus was characterized by a newly emerged '*party secretary psychology*' (CLO,55), but he was optimistic that the infection could be cured. Was the situation hopeless?

Not at all! The present critical period... will teach a good deal to the majority of the apparatus workers and will get them to abandon most of their errors. (CLO,69)

Trotsky's assessment was based on the idea that a change in administrators' methods and habits of mind could be made through example and teaching, and that bad habits could soon be corrected. But the practical remedy that he had already recommended was unlikely to have improved his popularity. In April 1923, Trotsky declared in *Pravda*:

An exemplary 'calendar program' would be to single out a hundred civil servants... a hundred who showed a rooted contempt in their duties for the working masses, and publicly, perhaps by trial, chuck them out of the state machine, so that they could never come back again. It would be a good beginning. [13]

His imperious optimism does not seem to be borne up by that side of his analysis which examined the reasons for the bureaucratic infection. He argued that there were three elements in this process. One concerned bad administrative habits which had survived the war communism period. But Trotsky also suggested that bureaucratism was the result of the merging of the Bolshevik Party with the Soviet state, and of the general lack of economic development compounded by international isolation.

Trotsky was chiefly concerned at this stage with bad manners, which he thought reflected a feeling of superiority of Bolsheviks over the masses, or the failure to consider seriously the problems of ordinary people. During the period of war communism, this sort of rushed administrative behaviour was easily explained and to a large extent justifiable. But the present evil of bureaucratism, Trotsky wrote, 'is the result of the transference to the party of the methods and administrative manners accumulated during these last years' (CLO,70). This echoed the sentiment expressed in November 1923 by Evgenii Preobrazhensky, who declared that the Party had failed 'to liquidate the military methods' [14], and had actually intensified its bureaucratism. Trotsky believed that during war communism, the secretarial apparatus had raised itself above the Party. Now, however, '*the party must subordinate to itself its own apparatus* without

16

for a moment ceasing to be a centralised organization' (CLO,124). The excessive centralism of the earlier years had served its purpose and had become a brake on the development of the Party.

But there was a general problem with Trotsky's argument. If certain measures had been responses to certain exceptional situations, and if those situations had now ended, to what should the Party 'return'? What was 'normal' or 'usual' for Bolshevism (and how, the Old Guard might have asked, would Trotsky know anyway)? Everything after the October Revolution was for the Soviet state 'exceptional', perhaps even the so-called flowering of democracy in the Bolshevik Party during the Civil War.

What had caused the deterioration in relations between the Party apparatus and the masses? Was it just the persistence of the haughtiness produced by war communism, or were there more fundamental reasons? Trotsky hinted at the latter by arguing that 'The state apparatus is the most important source of bureaucratism' (CLO,91) since 'the whole daily bureaucratic practice of the Soviet state... infiltrates the party apparatus' (CLO,78). This position was developed earlier by Lenin, who feared that inextricable links had sprung up between state and Party.

The merging of the Party with the state apparatus was a problem freely aired at the Eleventh Party Congress in 1922, [15] but the problems that it gave rise to were not fully understood. In his political report to that Congress, Lenin had suggested that the problem was one of political control, and that the bureaucracy—largely inherited from Tsarist times—had too much power:

If we take Moscow with its 4,700 Communists in responsible positions, and if we take that huge bureaucratic machine, that gigantic heap, we must ask: who is directing whom?... To tell the truth, they [the Communists] are not directing, they are being directed. [16]

Trotsky used this line of attack in his campaign against the triumvirate. The predominance of bureaucratic habits and attitudes among Communist administrators, of bureaucratism, had weakened political control over the bureaucracy.

The state-Party relationship had grown closer and the two became less distinguishable after the Revolution. 'Before the end of Lenin's life... the authority of the party over every aspect of policy and every branch of administration had been openly recognized and proclaimed', wrote Carr. [17] Here were the seeds of bureaucratism, Trotsky thought. In the *New Course*, he put the problem thus: the proletariat exercises its leadership over the state through the Communist Party.

17

The whole question is to realise this leadership without merging into the bureaucratic apparatus of the state, in order not to be exposed to a bureaucratic degeneration. (CLO,76–7)

Party members who found themselves in a hierarchy of relations to each other and to citizens in the state apparatus are likely, Trotsky implied, to look at problems from the administrative perspective of state functionaries. He declared that the whole Party, and not individual administrators, should exercise its leadership over every sector of the state apparatus.

The final source of bureaucratism identified by Trotsky's early analyses may be described as 'economic'. While this factor was to play a significant role in his later thought, it is mentioned only in passing in the *New Course*:

The source of bureaucratism resides in the growing concentration of the party's attention and efforts upon the governmental institutions and apparatuses, *and in the slowness of the development of industry.* (CLO,75; my emphasis)

Not only were Party members adopting bad habits and a bureaucratic outlook by being exposed to the cares of state administration, but the economic backwardness of Russia prolonged the very existence of the state. Trotsky suggested that the state inevitably had a bureaucratizing influence upon its functionaries, and therefore that its abolition would mean the end of bureaucratism; until then, the Party should remain aloof from the state.

Backwardness by itself, Trotsky argued in a collection of his articles entitled *Literature and Revolution*, bred bad manners. That Russia was still backward meant that Party members had to be vigilant to avoid contamination. He advocated economic development, in which the advancement of international revolution was decisive, to improve the Party's social composition. If more proletarians were enrolled, he held, the proletarian outlook of its leaders would be restored. To combat the specific weight of state and Party functionaries—those who had been cut adrift from ordinary workers—necessitated 'a substantial economic progress, a strong impulsion to industrial life, and a constant flow of manual workers into the party' (CLO,73). The unfortunate phrase adopted by his opponent Bukharin in 1925, that the Soviet Union should industrialize even if only 'at a snail's pace', was grist to Trotsky's theoretical mill.

But why should Trotsky have begun at this moment a campaign against bureaucratism? Despite the cogency of much of his analysis, there seems to have been a more directly political motive, concerned with Trotsky's position in the Bolshevik leadership, and with his defeat over the issue of economic policy. Trotsky's political predicament was, for him, symptomatic of Bolshevism's ails. In summary, he argued that bureaucratism was not just

the aggregate of the bad habits of officeholders. Bureaucratism is a social phenomenon in that it is a definite system of administration.... Its profound causes lie in the heterogeneity of society, the difference between the daily and the fundamental interests of various groups of the population. Bureaucratism is complicated by the lack of culture among the broad masses. With us, the essential source of bureaucratism resides in the necessity of creating and sustaining a state apparatus that unites the interests of the proletariat and those of the peasantry. (CLO,91–2)

For Trotsky, the profound causes of bureaucratism are social; bureaucratism is not simply a question of bad habits. The workers' state, he argued, still had to accommodate the interests of the peasantry.

States, Trotsky implied, necessarily give rise to bad administrative manners because of their hierarchical organization. But haughtiness should not creep into relations between Bolsheviks, he maintained, even if they were state functionaries. Trotsky did not propose a change in administrative procedures, but insisted that the Party must remain separate, and that Party consciousness must not be subordinated to administrative consciousness. Yet he conceded that

the party apparatus goes more and more into the details of the tasks of the Soviet apparatus, lives the life of its day-to-day cares, [and] lets itself be influenced increasingly by it.... (CLO,77)

It was not just a question of transferring the methods of state administration into the workings of the Party organization, as Trotsky seemed to indicate (CLO,78), but a merging of the apparatuses of the two. Bureaucratic administration is based on knowledge, as Max Weber pointed out. [18] Because of Russia's general cultural backwardness, and because administration is not quite so simple a matter as Lenin had intimated in his *The State and Revolution*, a bureaucracy re-formed after the October Revolution, using many of the professional personnel of the Tsarist bureaucracy.

In relation to administration in general, both Lenin and Trotsky had, at times, rather simple conceptions. Lenin declared that workers would be drawn into the everyday work of state administration, for the functions of the transitional state would be reduced, as he put it, 'to a comparatively simple system of *book-keeping*, which any literate person can do'. [19] Trotsky concurred:

I consider that in all areas of life and creative work certain common methods are applied. In the area of administration, a good administrator of a

19

factory or plant will also be a good military administrator. The methods of administration, in general and on the whole, are identical. Human logic is applied in much the same way in the military field as in others: accuracy, persistence, these are the qualities necessary to any field where people wish to build, to create, to learn. [20]

The division of labour represented by an ordinary bureaucracy, according to Lenin and Trotsky, could be broken down by workers taking various bureaucratic offices in rotation. Nevertheless, a bureaucracy was still considered necessary at first: one that was helping to undermine its own basis by educating workers in these 'simple' functions of administration. Such a bureaucracy would have been under the control of the Bolshevik Party, and operating in the interests of the workers, not in its own interests.

The realities of power, however, were more complex. Bolshevik cadres staffed various state institutions. Yet Lenin became concerned about the threat from the bureaucracy—not from the changes which may have been undergone by his Bolsheviks in administration, but by the use of 'bourgeois' specialists (which the Bolsheviks had found essential). Near the end of his life, he expressed the fear that bureaucratic methods were becoming more widespread because the old Tsarist state apparatus had not been smashed by the Revolution. [21] Marx himself had warned the German liberals in 1848 that the old bureaucracy had not been destroyed and was regaining its strength to attempt a return to monarchy.

A commissariat was established to counter 'bureaucratism and corruption in Soviet institutions'. Following the Eighth Party Congress (March 1919) the People's Commissariat of State Control was formed. In 1920 it became the People's Commissariat of Workers' and Peasants' Inspection, or Rabkrin. After Lenin's frank remarks on the state bureaucracy at the Eleventh Party Congress in 1922, he proposed that Rabkrin should extend its regulatory functions. [22] This provoked a sharp response from Trotsky, who thought little of the work and staff of the Inspectorate. [23] But he also suggested that the problem should be tackled in different ways:

the criterion of a good apparatus can only be achieved by means of consistent, uninterrupted, day-to-day efforts, pressure, instructions, correction, etc. [24]

rather than through an external 'control' institution. Trotsky's allusion to the futility of administrative control over the administration seems unique in the writings of this period, yet it was not clear from where the above-mentioned pressures were to emanate. This is a problem which exercised the Chinese communists some years later, and which they tried to countervail by implementing 'dual rule', integrating Party units at every level of the vertical chain of administrative command. [25] But the question of political control over bureaucracy is different from that of doing away with bureaucracy itself.

Within a few months of his proposal to strengthen Rabkrin, Lenin had changed his opinion of the agency. His last two articles, especially 'Better Fewer, But Better', were attacks on its functioning. By this time Lenin had concluded that 'We have bureaucrats in our Party offices as well as in Soviet offices'. [26] It is not clear here whether Lenin believed that the Bolshevik Party had become a bureaucratic organization, or whether Party members had taken over bureaucratic manners from participating in the state apparatus. Lenin recognized that the Party and state apparatuses were merging. As early as 1921, he wrote: 'As the governing party we could not help fusing the Soviet "authorities" with the party "authorities"—with us they are fused and they will be'. [27] The Party made state policy; the state commissariats were ultimately responsible to its Central Control Commission; and Party members worked in concert in all the institutions of the state. The Party exercised complete formal control. The Soviets were, in effect, replaced by the Party.

One of the most significant features of Trotsky's analysis in the *New Course* is the omission of any discussion, or even mention, of a Party bureaucracy: bureaucratism was the threat. Trotsky was not against bureaucracy in the transitional state as such. Around 1920, he had declared that 'we suffer not so much from the bad sides of bureaucracy, as chiefly from the fact that we have not yet assimilated the many good sides'. [28] Lenin himself, many years earlier, had described bureaucracy (as centralism and subordination of lower to higher levels) as 'the organizational principle of revolutionary Social-Democracy'. [29] But when describing the Party hierarchy in 1923–24, Trotsky used the more cautious and less pejorative term 'apparatus'. It was 'bureaucratism in the... party apparatus' (CLO,92), 'the methods of the "apparatus"' (CLO,92), 'the general policy of the apparatus... its bureaucratic tendency' (CLO,72) against which he warned.

Bureaucracy engenders, and is based upon, bureaucratic behaviour: acceptable forms of operation which stress accuracy and thoroughness. Bureaucracy used in this neutral sense means a certain form of acceptable administration. The 'ethos' of the bureaucrat centres on adequately fulfilling his assigned tasks. Bureaucratism, in the sense in which it was employed by Trotsky, had another mean-

21

ing. Instead of acceptable administration, bureaucratism signified the unacceptable aspects of bureaucracy: corruption and inefficiency, its becoming a power serving its own interests, and particularly the development of a more ambitious outlook—a 'world view', in fact— rather than the professional ethos sketched above. The assimilation of Party leaders into the bureaucracy played an important role in this transformation, Trotsky implied. Yet the tenor of the *New Course* suggests that he did not believe that the Party apparatus had become a bureaucracy. Not until many years later did he mention bureaucracy in this regard. His private notes on the Leningrad Opposition (led by Zinoviev, chairman of the Comintern and President of the Leningrad Soviet), in October 1925, continue to express concern over the *apparatus* and its deterioration; Trotsky still believed that the process was reversible:

The extraordinary difficulty... in determining the real class essence of the differences is engendered by the absolutely unprecedented role of the party apparatus; in this respect it has gone far beyond what existed even a year ago. (CLO,285)

By exposing bureaucratism and the abuse of bureaucratic power, Trotsky hoped to stem the growth of a self-serving bureaucracy. 'What is needed', he advised, is that 'this old generation should change its orientation' (CLO,73).

To acknowledge the existence of a Party bureaucracy would have been to admit the identity of the Party, the proletariat's political vanguard, with the repressive apparatus of the state, and to announce the end of Party democracy. But was the apparatus already a bureaucracy? In the opening pages of his *New Course*, Trotsky implied that it was. In his 'first letter' to the Central Committee, Trotsky wrote: 'the *bureaucratization of the party apparatus* has reached unheardof proportions through the application of the methods of secretarial selection' (CLO,56). Party secretaries, Trotsky argued, had become independent of their local cells since their position depended upon appointment rather than election. 'Organized from the top down, the secretarial apparatus has, in an increasingly autonomous fashion, been gathering "all the strings into its own hands"' (CLO,55).

Trotsky's criticisms of 'secretarial bureaucratism' suggest that not merely the issue of bad manners was at stake, but that bad manners represented the growth of a new, and increasingly bolder, social stratum:

There is no doubt that the chairmen of the regional committees or the divisional commissars, whatever their social origin, represent a definite social type, regardless of their individual origin. During these six years fairly

22

stable social groupings have been formed in the Soviet regime. (CLO,74) But Trotsky was not, at this stage, more explicit about a bureaucracy within the Party. In later writings, he predated its emergence. In 1936, for example, he argued that 'By freeing the bureaucracy from the control of the proletarian vanguard, the "Leninist Levy" dealt a death blow to the party of Lenin' (RB,98). Unable on grounds of political expediency to oppose this political expedient, and perhaps hoping that it would assist his campaign, Trotsky nevertheless saw it later as a decisive ploy on the part of the apparatus to dilute the proletarian character of the Party.

Trotsky's campaign against bureaucratization was allied to an economic programme. The ideas of planning, the New Economic Policy, and of the relations between workers and peasants, as well as the means to finance industrialization were issues hotly debated in the highest ranks of the Party. Each attracted changing coalitions of forces. Trotsky's isolation in the Politburo, and Lenin's effective absence after mid-1922 meant the end of any degree of fair play for Trotsky's proposals. The NEP created problems for the Bolsheviks, just as war communism had done. Wealthy peasants began to appear, while food prices increased in the cities. There seemed to be an inverse relation between the interests of workers and peasants. While 'the new attitude to the peasant was the foundation of NEP' [30], it had important effects on industry as well. Decentralization was accompanied by new accounting procedures; the 'trust' became the basic level economic accounting unit. [31] Private management returned to some previously nationalized industries, but the Party argued that the state controlled the 'commanding heights' of the economy. [32] Market principles meant that state industry had to accept 'commercial principles', and profit became a motive for production once more. In this situation Trotsky stressed the imperative need for centralized planning and rapid industrialization.

The immediate prelude to the Left Opposition's campaign against bureaucratization was an economic crisis created by the growing gap in the prices of industrial *vis-à-vis* agricultural products. During 1923 industrial prices rose much more quickly than those in the agricultural sector. As Alec Nove explained, 'by October 1923, when the "scissors crisis" reached its peak [industrial and agricultural prices having been depicted as the blades of a pair of scissors], industrial prices were three times higher, relative to agricultural prices, than they had been before the [first world] war'. [33] Peasants became wary of marketing their products because of the unfavourable terms of trade between city and country. Threatening to rupture the

23

smytchka, or link, between worker and peasant on which the life of the early Soviet republic depended, the 'scissors' crisis led to friction within the Bolshevik Party over which course of action to take. Trotsky advocated an acceleration of the tempo of industrial development.

To argue for industrialization and a reduction in bureaucracy in the same breath, an unstated theme in the *New Course* and all other documents by Trotsky in the 1920s, appears to be self-defeating. The idea is implicit in the *New Course*, but was clearly expressed ten years later by Trotsky's follower, Max Shachtman:

The program for restoring workers' democracy and eliminating the bureaucratic deformities which were beginning to cripple the party and the dictatorship, had another important aspect. From the very beginning, it was coupled with the perspective of speeding up the industrialization of economically backward Russia. [34]

In the *New Course*, Trotsky was decidedly more cautious:

The struggle against the bureaucratism of the state apparatus is an exceptionally important but prolonged task, one that runs more or less parallel to our other fundamental tasks—economic reconstruction and the elevation of the cultural level of the masses. (CLO,92)

Generally the Bolsheviks had seen the solution to bureaucracy in terms of a more direct participation by the masses in state functions. [35] But to be equipped to handle such tasks required a rise in the level of culture, [36] particularly education. Lenin had written that the workers 'would like to build a better apparatus for us, but they do not know how.... They have not yet developed the culture required for this'. [37] This was the point of Trotsky's emphasis on industrialization. The relation between backwardness and bureaucratization was not a simple one in Trotsky's view. It led, as we have seen, to state functions being taken over by specialists, to a professional bureaucracy; and to an attitude of superiority and haughtiness which seemed to have infected the Party.

In conjunction with his stress on industrialization, Trotsky raised the question of the social composition of the Party, a question to which he adverted in later years. Citing the small proportion of Party members who were workers, [38] and the increasing numbers of ex-Socialist Revolutionaries and ex-Mensheviks who occupied significant Party posts, Trotsky attributed the Party crisis to these 'ex-es' and other alien class elements. In short, industrialization was heralded as the way to increase the proletarian proportion of the Party, and thus overcome bureaucratization. The Lenin Levy, however, revealed that new members were more easily manipulated than the old. Proletarian

24

membership before the Revolution had never guaranteed the Party's proletarian credentials, and few of the Old Bolsheviks were sons of the working class.

Furthermore, the industrialization which Trotsky advocated, and which eventually got underway in the 1930s, gave rise to a vast expansion of managerial, engineering, technical and scientific personnel, an increase in the division of labour and in the managerial hierarchy. The premium placed on technology and science, refracted through state ownership, represented a strong force in the direction of bureaucratization. R.V. Daniels, for example, argued that

The first requirement of industrial life... is the bureaucratic and hierarchical organisation of specialists. Industry and its ancillary services require authority in order to direct large-scale operations quickly and effectively; discipline so that every one on every level fulfils his responsibilities; technical skill appropriate to each level, with a high degree of division of labour.... [39]

Trotsky's proposals, in fact, would have made the problems of bureaucracy and the consequent dangers of bureaucratism more acute. But his campaign was really aimed against bureaucratism, against the moral degeneration of the proletarian vanguard.

The Thirteenth Party Congress of May 1924, ratifying the decision of the conference four months earlier, brought to an end the New Course discussion and, with it, the Left Opposition. In general, the Opposition had enjoyed little success other than in Moscow and mainly amongst students. With the Lenin Levy, membership of the Party increased by about forty percent. According to Daniels, it was 'swamped... with political neophytes firmly under the control of the secretarial hierarchy'. [40] If it had not done so before, the Party apparatus had consolidated its control. Trotsky surrendered, but he refused to renounce his views, as Zinoviev (in an unprecedented move) demanded (CLO,161).

Trotsky returned to the fray in September 1924, having penned 'The Lessons of October' as a preface to his collected writings and speeches of 1917, then being published. Seeking to discredit some of the Party's most esteemed leaders, especially for their undistinguished or obstructive roles in the Revolution, the essay served only to isolate Trotsky further, as a torrent of material struck back at the 'misdeeds' of his own career. Lenin's widow, Krupskaya, summed up the feelings of those who took issue with this account of October (and who did not simply begin to falsify history by conjuring up the spectre of 'Trotskyism'): 'Marxist analysis was never Comrade Trotsky's strong point'. [41]

For more than a year afterwards Trotsky remained silent and aloof—engrossing himself in French novels during Central Committee meetings [42]—while the Leningrad Opposition challenged Stalin and was defeated. Zinoviev sought *rapprochement* with Trotsky, and by April 1926 they had formed the United Opposition. Officially proclaimed in July, after a secret meeting of oppositionists had been uncovered, it issued 'The Declaration of the Thirteen'. The *New Course* was a unique oppositional document because of its length and circulation; after 1924 we must look to more cryptic declarations for information about Trotsky's response to bureaucratization. The 'Declaration' blamed bureaucratism for divisions within the Party. Bureaucratic caution and the suppression of criticism within the Comintern were cited as the causes of recent errors, involving especially the Anglo-Russian Trade Union Unity Committee. [43]

We address ourselves to the plenum of the Central Committee with the proposal that with our common efforts we restore a party regime which will permit the decision of all disputed questions in full conformity with all the traditions of the party.... Only on this foundation is party democracy possible. [44]

Such criticism was combined, as always, with a programme for industrialization: 'Everything should be subordinated to this task'. [45]

But the United Opposition was no more successful in getting its platform accepted by the Party than was the Left Opposition before it. It fragmented at the Fifteenth Party Congress in 1927, when Zinoviev yielded to the Party leadership and recanted. Many Oppositionists were soon expelled from the Party, or signed statements of recantation. Leading Trotskyists who continued to defy the leadership were offered minor administrative posts in remote sections of the Soviet Union even before the end of 1927. Trotsky himself was destined for Astrakhan when he was charged by the secret police, the GPU, with counter-revolutionary activity and deported to Alma Ata, Turkestan. There, in isolation, he spent the next year until he was exiled from the USSR in February 1929.

The focus of the debates of the 1920s was the Party. If he could prevent the bureaucratization of the Party (and chiefly the Old Guard), Trotsky held, then the health of the regime would remain intact. The Party, according to him, had become infected with bureaucratism, and this was a measure of its differentiation from the actual proletariat and its interests, and all of this in turn was reflected in a disastrous economic policy which nurtured the rich peasant. The catchwords of Trotsky's campaign were 'democracy' and 'bureaucratization'. His stress on democracy seems to echo his condemnation, in 1903, of Lenin's organizational formula of democratic centralism as leading to 'substitutionism':

The party organization at first substitutes itself for the party as a whole; then the Central Committee substitutes itself for the organization; and finally a single 'dictator' substitutes himself for the Central Committee.... [46]

But however apposite this early criticism, Trotsky had since accepted that the will of the Party and the proletariat could be embodied in a single man, and ridiculed 'formal' democracy. After uniting with the Bolsheviks in 1917, he became a staunch centralist, who accepted the logic of, and helped to implement, 'substitutionism'. His concern now was with the character of the substitutes.

There is room for argument about the internal Party regime until Lenin's death. His influence, however, was decisive. Lenin would not allow the Bolshevik leaders, besides himself, to determine a decision. But he also proposed a ban on factions within the Party at the Tenth Congress in March 1921. Trotsky claimed that this ban was exceptional and temporary (RB,96), but this was not clear at the time. While unity was deemed essential, and its disruption rewarded with 'immediate and unconditional expulsion', the resolution was tempered with Lenin's words:

We cannot deprive the party and the members of the Central Committee of the right to turn to the party, if a basic question evokes dissension.... We haven't the power to suppress this. [47]

Lenin declared that they had not the *power* to suppress an appeal to the Party; not that they had not the right. The resolution, with its self-perpetuating logic ('It was enough of them [the Left Oppositionists] to speak up for a revision of the rules to lay themselves open to the accusation that they had already violated them', Deutscher explained [48]), became the whip with which the triumvirate flailed the Opposition, even if its own existence was a form of factionalism.

Trotsky had urged that this was a period in which the democratic character of democratic centralism must be emphasized:

The party is essentially a democratic organization, that is, a collectivity which decides upon its road by the thought and the will of all its members. (CLO,70)

It was also, however, a direct attack on the Old Guard, in which appeals to a particular kind of democracy were expedient. To the Old Bolsheviks, his behaviour must have seemed grossly disloyal to them and to Bolshevism itself, which had never been at the whim of its members.

Just as in his 1923 articles on 'Problems of Everyday Life' Trotsky exhorted the Russian people to do better—to desist from swearing, to be punctual, to attend diligently to small matters—so in his campaign against bureaucratism he exhorted Party members and leaders to do better. Howe wrote: 'Trotsky the preacher, Trotsky the schoolmaster, Trotsky the moralist: how odd, how priggish, how (at times) charming!' [49] But his Party colleagues did not think it so charming. Trotsky considered having wine in the Kremlin in 1919 as a 'softening' of habits. [50] He fell out with his brother-in-law, Kamenev, because his table was laden with fine foods at a time of general hardship. Leadership, Trotsky believed, involved setting an example for others to follow; bureaucratism threatened to undermine the moral authority of the Bolsheviks and to divert them from their goal. The struggle against bureaucratism had to be waged relentlessly, he explained, 'by word and deed, by propaganda, and higher standards, by exhortation, and by calling individuals to account for their behaviour'. [51] The Party's links with the state apparatus were the chief source of his concern:

If a party member has become so 'specialized' in his departmental work that he has lost his moral link with the party, there is no point in his remaining in the party.... The communist who is in danger of suffering such a degeneration must be pulled up with a jerk in good time. [52]

Only seven months after he published these lines, Trotsky concluded that most of the Party needed to be 'pulled up with a jerk', and opened his 'New Course' campaign.

As early as June 1923, Trotsky had canvassed the possibility of a restoration of capitalism in Russia 'if we, as a party, sell out or blunder in a historically significant way'. [53] Trotsky was remarkably and, for a Leninist, uncharacteristically alive to theoretical possibilities. If he raised here the issue of a restoration of capitalism in Russia, in 1939 he would question the validity of historical materialism. In neither case did he concede the possibility; rather, they were designed to shock people into thinking out the consequences of their positions. In 1923, he relied on the character of the Bolsheviks to sustain his faith in the socialist future of Russia:

The revolutionists of our epoch... possess their own special psychological characteristics, qualities of intellect and will. [54]

On their sturdiness, he believed, lay the fate of the Revolution.

Trotsky worked within, and accepted, the framework of one-party rule. He did not ask whether the proletarian policy of the Soviet state (for this, after all, was what the debate was all about) might be better guaranteed by allowing freedom of Soviet parties. His remarks about bureaucratization were more about the separation of the Party leadership from the proletariat than about organizational procedures and the struggle against bureaucracy itself. The Party, Trotsky believed, had begun to adopt a bureaucratic approach towards the proletariat. He campaigned to preserve its proletarian credentials by putting his policies into effect, and that meant defeating the existing leadership. Trotsky assumed that when proletarians entered the Party they would naturally support his policy.

Trotsky's campaign failed for many reasons. First, because he did not realize the extent of resentment towards him among the Party leaders; his self-confidence and asceticism only reinforced long-standing political enmity. Second, because although his was a political campaign against the existing leadership clique, he turned it into a diffuse appeal for democratization and against bureaucratization, which none of his opponents ever openly challenged. Trotsky was unskilled as a politician. Third, he was a victim of procedures and a style of politics that he himself had endorsed and helped to implement. Trotsky's campaign did, however, highlight the fact that in one-party states the ruling party is subject to all sorts of unforeseen pressures, even though his proposals amount simply to a determination to resist those pressures.

3

THE TRIAL

Expelled from the Soviet Union, Trotsky spent the remainder of his life as an itinerant critic of Soviet policy. His followers and family in the USSR and around the world were hounded by agents of Stalin, and Trotsky himself was eventually assassinated. During his last years, years of the Great Depression, of Stalin's programme of intensified industrialization and bloody collectivization of agriculture, and of the rise of Nazism, Trotsky finalized his analysis of the Soviet state. From 1929 to 1933, he put the Stalin leadership on trial. His verdict: that Bolshevism was dead in the Soviet Communist Party and the Communist International.

In the Soviet Union, Stalin's 'left turn' in economic policies—towards industrialization and collectivization—began to decimate the Trotskyists who had been dispersed after the Fifteenth Congress. Stalin appeared to have adopted the economic platform of the Opposition and thus its *raison d'être*. Was this not the 'proletarian policy' Trotsky had long advocated? In July 1929, Preobrazhensky, Karl Radek, Ivan Smilga and four hundred others surrendered to Stalin. They were followed in November by Ivan Smirnov and hundreds more. Christian Rakovsky was the only leading Oppositionist to hold out until early in 1934. Those who 'surrendered' met with scorn from Trotsky; he dismissed them as 'dead souls' (TW 1929,198), overlooking the possibility that his earlier aloofness from party ties better prepared him for excommunication. To the stalwarts, he explained that there were still fundamental differences separating the Opposition from Stalin; only at the surface was there any agreement.

The leadership, even after having absorbed officially a good number of our *tactical* deductions, still maintains the *strategic* principles from which yesterday's right-centre tactic emerged. (TW 1929,327)

In fact, Trotsky attributed whatever good came from the Stalin leadership to the pressure of the Opposition:

What has produced the left twitch of the apparatus? *Our* attack, *our* irreconcilability, the growth of *our* influence, the courage of *our* cadres. (TW 1929,162)

But Trotsky was out of touch with the sentiments of his Soviet followers. That many Oppositionists renounced him serves to highlight not just the difficulties of exile, but also the basic issue as they perceived it: how policy was decided was secondary to its 'proletarian' character. The differences between the remaining Oppositionists and the Party were underlined at the end of 1929 when Jacob Blumkin, a GPU official and Oppositionist sympathiser (not at all an unusual combination), was executed after visiting Trotsky in exile. Deutscher claimed that Blumkin 'was the first party member on whom capital punishment was inflicted for an inner party offence, an offence no graver than being in contact with Trotsky'; [1] yet Trotsky was now considered to be a class enemy, not a wayward Bolshevik.

To differentiate his policy from Stalin's, Trotsky focused on the *methods* of industrialization and collectivization, criticizing them as adventurist and ultra-left. The new course in the Soviet economy was just as bad, he suggested, as the old (TW 1930,107). Having been accused of 'underestimating the peasantry' early in the 1920s, on account of his industrialization proposals, Trotsky argued now that collectivization should be more gradual. To prevent the reappearance of the *kulaks*, or rich peasants, 'an industrial and cultural revolution is necessary' (TW 1930,112).

Although a hallmark of bureaucratic administration is predictability, the sudden left turn in Soviet economic policy was followed by a change in foreign policy. It was argued that the 'Third Period' was on the historical agenda: the period of the destruction of capitalism, and the radicalization of the masses. Molotov declared in 1929 that 'we have entered with both feet into the realm of *most tremendous revolutionary events* of international significance' (cited TW 1930,52). Trotsky, however, argued that this was a ruse to discourage revolution, and to preserve world peace so that Stalin could build 'Socialism in One Country'. After the Communist International incorporated the doctrine of 'Socialism in One Country' into its 1928 programme, Trotsky held that its parties had become diplomatic pawns of the Soviet state. 'Their mission' he concluded, 'is to protect the USSR from intervention and not to fight for the conquest of power' [2]—a prognosis he believed was fully confirmed by the events of the 1930s.

Stressing the international nature of socialism was another component of the argument he was developing about the dangers to the Soviet state:

The maintenance of the proletarian revolution within a national framework can only be a provisional state of affairs.... In an isolated proletarian dictatorship, the internal and external contradictions grow inevitably along

31

with the successes achieved. If it remains isolated, the proletarian state must finally fall victim to these contradictions. [3]

The debate over 'Socialism in One Country', begun in Russia around 1924, shows Trotsky the politician at his most inept. The precise meaning of the doctrine was never clear, but it was tactically useful in the struggle against Trotsky and Trotskyism (which was associated with the idea of 'Permanent Revolution'), and it was also useful for the masses. Robert Day rightly argues that

Socialism in One Country was more than a slogan or even an economic programme: it was a psychological watershed in the history of the revolution.... The new doctrine helped to restore the sense of mission which had been lost in 1921. [4]

But Trotsky saw it as an enervating doctrine. He found hardship bracing. Of the appalling conditions endured by Oppositionists in exile in the USSR, he reflected: 'It is only in this way that the selection and tempering of revolutionaries is produced' (TW 1929,199). Devotion and sacrifice were the traits of a revolutionary (TW 1929,192). Suffering sorted out the revolutionaries from the opportunists and others. After first denying that his theory of Permanent Revolution had anything to do with the debate over Socialism in One Country, Trotsky then supplemented his theory and made it the basis of 'Trotskyism'. For revolutionaries, there could be no relaxation.

Trotsky's attention was increasingly drawn to the rise of Nazism in Germany. He was alarmed that Communists refused to cooperate with the reformist Social Democrats to stop the Nazis. He warned that by dubbing social democrats 'social fascists', and claiming that they were more dangerous than fascists, the Comintern disarmed the workers against the real dangers of fascism (TW 1930,140). His forecasts of war if Hitler came to power proved remarkably accurate (TW 1932,76). Trotsky held that Nazism could be defeated if only the Communist Party would adopt the tactics he advocated. Like most problems, he believed that one need simply apply correct leadership. A united front between the Communist and Socialist Parties, he argued, was the only immediate solution. Such a front may not have been altogether helpless in repulsing the Nazis, but there is no certainty that it would have succeeded. Trotsky's remarks on Soviet foreign policy in general incorporate a logical error. Although he saw Soviet failures as confirmation of his own approach, there could be no conclusive test of this. His analysis of Nazism itself was perhaps his truly great achievement in exile, yet Trotsky was ridiculed and abused. As late as September 1932, Ernest Thaelman, a leader of the German Communist Party (KPD), declared:

This is the theory of an utterly bankrupt fascist and counter-revolutionary. This is indeed the worst, the most dangerous, and the most criminal theory that Trotsky has construed in these last years of his counter-revolutionary propaganda. [5]

On 30 January 1933, Hitler became Chancellor of Germany. A month later the organizations of the German working class, its parties and trade unions, had been destroyed. Early in March 1933, Trotsky communicated his verdict to his colleagues: 'The KPD today represents a corpse' (TW 1932–33,137). This position was made public soon after, in an article entitled 'The Tragedy of the German Proletariat':

If the German proletariat found itself impotent, disarmed and paralysed at the moment of its greatest historical test, the direct and immediate blame falls upon the leadership of the post-Leninist Comintern.... [6]

Trotsky blamed the Soviet leadership for the German catastrophe. Its foreign policy was now a litmus test of the condition of the USSR. He went on:

Stalinism in Germany has had its 4 August.... The official German Communist Party is doomed.... German communism can be reborn only on a new basis and with a new leadership.... The German proletariat will rise again, Stalinism—never. [7]

Henceforth, the task of German Trotskyists was not to remain loyal oppositionists to the KPD, a faction (albeit expelled) of a dead party. They must construct a new party, in the hope that other sections of the Comintern would respond to the German defeat by abandoning Stalinism. 'It is not a question of the creation of the Fourth International' Trotsky advised, 'but of salvaging the Third' (TW 1932–33,138). But Moscow endorsed the KPD's course and the other sections duly complied. (In 1935, the KPD policy was officially repudiated, and the German leaders were made scapegoats for the defeat of 1933.) For Trotsky, the Comintern was damned. In July 1933, he declared that a Fourth International was necessary. The parties of the Comintern could no longer be reformed:

An organization which was not roused by the thunder of fascism and which submits docilely to such outrageous acts of the bureaucracy demonstrates thereby that it is dead and that nothing can ever revive it. (TW 1932–33,305)

The collapse of the KPD had squarely posed the problem, for Trotsky, of the Third International; the 'collapse' of the Third International posed the problem of the Soviet Union. 'Foreign policy is everywhere and always a continuation of domestic policy' (RB,186), he later remarked. In the wake of the German events, Trotsky was uncertain of the proper course to follow within the USSR; but he never doubted its post-capitalist status. In July 1933, he set out the parameters for an analysis of the Soviet regime which he would later develop in *The Revolution Betrayed*:

The October Revolution, with the Bolshevik Party at its head, created the workers' state. Now the Bolshevik Party no longer exists. But the fundamental social content of the October Revolution is still alive. The bureaucratic dictatorship, notwithstanding the technical successes achieved under it (against itself), greatly facilitates the possibility of the capitalist restoration, but luckily the point of a restoration has not yet been reached. With favourable internal and, above all, international conditions, the edifice of the workers' state can be regenerated on the social foundations of the Soviet Union without a new revolution. (TW 1933–34,20)

Trotsky's basic commitment was to the idea that the USSR was created and remained a workers' state, characterized by nationalized means of production and a state monopoly of foreign trade. By October 1933, he had decided that his followers should attempt to establish a new party inside the Soviet Union, to work for a political revolution against the ruling bureaucracy. He maintained that the collapse of the Comintern as a revolutionary organization did not signify the collapse of the dictatorship of the proletariat.

How, he asked, could a regime inaugurated by the great social upheaval of 1917 founder and return to capitalism without another such upheaval? 'He who asserts that the Soviet government has been *gradually* changed from proletarian to bourgeois is only, so to speak, running backwards the film of reformism' (TW 1933–34,103). Yet how could Bolshevism itself have gradually withered and died in Russia? The revolution of October 1917, according to Trotsky, had established the dictatorship of the proletariat, defined by its 'forms of property'. As long as these property forms remained—even though the 'bureaucracy has expropriated the proletariat politically... the proletariat remains the ruling class' (TW 1933–34,104). But how much had really been achieved by the October Revolution? Although he talked of the 'political expropriation of the proletariat' under Stalin, he really meant that the proletarian section of the Bolshevik Party (i.e., his section) had been expelled. Was the 'ruling bureaucracy' a 'ruling class'? Trotsky began to muster arguments to oppose the view that it was. Just as he had argued that the fascist bureaucracy was not a class, but a 'hireling of the bourgeoisie' (TW 1933–34,113), so the Soviet bureaucracy was not an independent class, no matter how significant the portion of social surplus value it consumed. Trotsky's analogy, however, raised some difficult questions. If the fascist

34

bureaucracy is merely a hireling, can it be fired? Is the Soviet bureaucracy the hireling of the proletariat? The extravagant consumption of the Soviet bureaucracy, Trotsky continued, derived not from its existence as a class with its own property relations, but occurred within the property relations established by October. It was therefore the duty of every revolutionary still to support the 'gains' of the Revolution (TW 1933-34,304).

As early as 1927, Stalin had challenged the Opposition to remove the bureaucracy by force (see RB,279). Trotsky now accepted the challenge.

After the experience of the last few years, it would be childish to suppose that the Stalinist bureaucracy can be removed by means of a party or soviet congress.... The bureaucracy can be compelled to yield power into the hands of the proletarian vanguard only by *force*. (TW 1933-34,117-18)

This is characteristic of his conception: Trotsky wanted Soviet power controlled by the proletarian *vanguard*, his own followers.

4

BOLSHEVISM BETRAYED

The Revolution Betrayed was the last major work that Trotsky finished, and he is perhaps best known for it. First published in 1936, it contains his most complete analysis of the Soviet Union. It was written partly in response to the claim of the newly adopted constitution of the USSR that socialism had already been established. [1] Trotsky believed that such a claim could not but diminish the appeals of socialism—just as Kautsky and other democratic socialists had earlier argued that the October Revolution would harm the cause of socialism. But he also wanted to set down a Marxist theory of the transition to socialism in light of the Soviet experience. The title itself is striking. Although the original manuscript had what is now the sub-title, 'What is the Soviet Union and Where is it going?', as the main title, and 'The Revolution Betrayed' as the sub-title, [2] the debut of the idea of 'betrayal' is consistent with his earlier work, despite the materialist terms in which the analysis is couched. The morality of leadership was Trotsky's underlying theme.

In the *New Course*, Trotsky made a bid for Party leadership, even if he offered the Bolsheviks only more years of hardship and devotion to duty. He earned respect and loyalty among those with whom he had direct contact in the Commissariat of War, but most had had enough of the privations of war communism. NEP and the doctrine of Socialism in One Country were both geared to an easing up from the heroic days. Trotsky's asceticism explains the paradox in his attitude towards the idea of socialism in a single country: when it was a question of political integrity, of defying the political and military odds, Trotsky supported it; when it became a question of slackening, of contentment and even indulgence, he opposed it. [3] In 1923, Trotsky thought the process of 'degeneration', as he even then called it, could be reversed by persuasion, but chiefly by his leadership of the Party and the implementation of his policies. In 1936, he believed that the Revolution had been betrayed, but not entirely overthrown. Only the removal of the Bolshevik Party could now return the regime to what he portrayed as its great days, before Lenin died. In 1923, he sought to preserve the proletarian essence of the Party; in 1936 he sought to overthrow the Stalinist bureaucracy.

Although *The Revolution Betrayed* analysed the ruling bureaucracy rather than 'bureaucratism', the remedy remained the same. Trotsky had begun to speak of a 'ruling bureaucracy' in the Soviet Union early in the 1930s. He now attempted not just to explain the growth of the Soviet bureaucracy, but its rise to power. These two, he believed, were separate problems; while the existence of bureaucracy was inevitable, the 'betrayal' of the Revolution by the Stalinists to the bureaucracy was not.

The growth of the Soviet bureaucracy did not accord with Marxist or Leninist expectations; Trotsky nevertheless looked to Marxist theory for guidance. The Marxist theory of the state has its problems, but Trotsky was not the man to recognize or to solve them. He merely built upon a conception of the state propounded chiefly by Lenin and Engels. According to Engels, the state was an organization appropriate to a certain stage of social development, class society; it did not exist before this stage, and it would not exist after it. It acted in the interests of the dominant or ruling class even though it often presented itself as a neutral arbiter between classes. Engels elaborated this view in *The Origin of the Family, Private Property and the State*, and concluded that the 'modern representative state is an instrument of exploitation of wage labour by capital'. [4] In his *The State and Revolution*, Lenin reaffirmed that the modern state, whatever its political form, was an instrument of the bourgeoisie. It was part of his campaign against those socialists who believed that modern, representative forms of government could be used by the proletariat to take and hold power. Lenin urged the overthrow of the 'bourgeois' state, and reaffirmed his belief in the need for a 'dictatorship of the proletariat', a state power to be used by the workers in the transition to a classless society. Although Lenin praised the organizational forms of the Soviets, contrasting them with parliaments, his support for them was a function of expediency. In July 1917, for example, he argued that the formerly correct slogan of 'All Power to the Soviets!' was no longer appropriate, and that the Bolsheviks must attempt to take power alone:

The aim of the insurrection can only be to transfer power to the proletariat, supported by the poor peasants, with a view to putting our Party programme into effect. [5]

Lenin and other Marxists focused on different aspects of the modern state to bolster their arguments. He and Engels saw the chief aspects of the state in its bureaucracy and its army: its administrative and repressive apparatuses. Other Marxists weighted more

37

heavily the legislative institutions of the democratic state. For Lenin, legislation was secondary in deciding the character of a state. The 'opportunists' were also discomforted by the idea of a dictatorship of the proletariat, which Lenin insisted was essential to a really revolutionary Marxism. But what precisely did this 'dictatorship' mean? How could a class rule? Lenin was adamant from his first sustained discussion of the concept that 'dictatorship' was the rule of the proletariat over its enemies: rule based on force, and unrestricted by any law. He did not detail its political organization. As long as the proletariat ruled through its vanguard, the proletarian nature of the state was guaranteed. What the state did, not its form of organization, was decisive for Lenin.

Lenin's neglect of political forms is apparent in *The State and Revolution*, for although he derided the 'bourgeois democracies' and praised the Soviets, he barely mentioned the role of the Party. Likewise, Trotsky's concern was not whether the regime was 'democratic' in the formal sense, but in whose interests the bureaucracy worked. Only the Party, he believed, could guarantee that the bureaucracy worked for the proletariat, and was in this sense 'democratic', and the health of the Party itself was at stake. Trotsky never seriously considered Soviet democracy as a solution to bureaucratization, except in so far as it might have been able to apply proletarian pressure to the Party and its leadership. But which parties should be allowed to exist under a Soviet democracy? Should they be alternative governments? Trotsky never conceded that any party but the Bolsheviks should be allowed to rule in the Soviet Union.

Bureaucracy was an early and continuing worry of the new Soviet regime while the army was not. Of these two key institutions, the army was controlled by the political commissars placed at its every level. Even when officers from the Tsarist army were brought in to assist, they were kept firmly in check. The loyalty of the Red Army to the Soviet regime was not in question, even though Trotsky was removed in 1925 from the post of Commissar of War because of Stalin's fear that he might seize power militarily.

The discussion of bureaucracy in the Soviet state highlighted a longstanding concern by the Bolsheviks about it. In *The State and Revolution*, Lenin declared that

There can be no thought of abolishing the bureaucracy at once, everywhere and completely. That is utopia. But to *smash* the old bureaucratic machine at once and to begin immediately to construct a new one that will permit to abolish gradually all bureaucracy—that is *not* utopia.... [6]

Lenin accepted the view that, as Engels put it, the state would 'wither

38

away'. In the meantime, it was necessary that a proletarian state take over from a bourgeois state. As Marx wrote,

Between capitalist and communist society lies the period of the revolutionary transformation of the one into the other. There corresponds to this also a political transition period in which the state can be nothing but *the revolutionary dictatorship of the proletariat.* [7]

But how was a 'proletarian bureaucracy', or a bureaucracy in the interests of the proletariat to be constructed, given the unfamiliarty of ordinary Russians with administration and the general level of education and culture? Lenin did not pose this problem seriously before the October Revolution. Instead, he depreciated it: administrative tasks were easy, anyone could do them. Reality, however, was different, and to avoid administrative collapse the Bolsheviks had to allow many Tsarist officials to return to their posts. Often these personnel were blamed for the problems of bureaucracy. They were, it was claimed, 'bourgeois survivals', and many became the targets of Stalin's political campaigns, deservedly or not. Like their efforts at political control in the Red Army, the Bolsheviks created inspectorates to try to control the bureaucracy, to ensure its loyalty.

Contrary to expectations, Trotsky found that the Soviet state was getting vastly bigger and more repressive. Indeed, reinforcement of the state apparatus, on the grounds that the bourgeoisie, having become smaller, grew more desperate in its resistance, had become official dogma (RB,62). [8] What was the real basis for the continued existence of bureaucracy? Trotsky found an answer of sorts in the writings of his mentors. Engels had argued that the state would no longer exist once 'class domination *and the struggle for individual existence*' disappeared (cited RB,52). The idea of backwardness came to Trotsky's rescue. If he had been among the first Marxists to stress the advantages of backwardness, he now complemented his conception with the idea (to use Thorstein Veblen's phrase) of 'the penalty for taking the lead'. The material basis of the Soviet state, he argued, could not yet remove this struggle for individual existence.

Trotsky also found support in Marx's works. 'Bourgeois law' Marx had written, 'is inevitable in the first phase of communist society'; [9] and Lenin interpreted this as meaning 'bourgeois law in regard to the distribution of *consumer* goods'. [10] The proletarian state must take charge of distribution. In effect, according to Lenin, the proletarian state would be a 'bourgeois state, without the bourgeoisie'. [11] Under the rule of the bourgeoisie, however, the market and not the state upholds this bourgeois 'law' of distribution, which returns to the producer a proportion of what he produces commensurate with his effort and skill in production, and not necessarily that which will satisfy his needs. Bourgeois law, in this sense, means to treat men equally, formally, and thus to treat them unequally, because each has different needs. Why and how the proletarian state would 'enforce' this 'law' is not clear. Bureaucracy itself might be considered the institutional embodiment of this 'necessity', in the first phase of socialism, to treat unequal men equally.

On the basis of these texts, Trotsky advanced the thesis that a post-capitalist state has a dual character:

socialistic, insofar as it defends social property in the means of production; bourgeois insofar as the distribution of life's goods is carried out with a capitalistic measure of value and all the consequences ensuing therefrom. (RB,54)

The upshot of this thesis is that the Soviet state continues to exist because of material necessity, and is not the product of struggle between antagonistic classes. This 'dual character' of the state becomes decisive only in a backward country on the path to socialism. The founders of Marxism had not seriously considered the ramifications of such an occurrence. How, then, does this 'bourgeois law of distribution', or the 'struggle for individual existence' affect the transitional state? The state, Trotsky argued, was required to 'regulate inequalities in the sphere of consumption' (RB,55), to accommodate privileged groups in defence, industry and science, whose existence was still necessary. The 'bourgeois law of distribution', as Trotsky put it, involves the valuing of some jobs higher than others, and rewarding them with better wage rates. Presumably this can create privileges of various sorts. As a result of this policy of 'bourgeois distribution', a caste of 'specialists in distribution' was established (RB,59). There is, he claimed, an 'iron necessity to give birth to and support a privileged minority so long as it is impossible to guarantee genuine equality' (RB,55), whatever 'genuine equality' might be.

Trotsky believed that his contribution to Marxist theory rested with the idea of the 'dual character' of the transitional state. While a tendency to bureaucracy would everywhere become manifest in the transition to socialism,

the poorer the society which issues from a revolution, the sterner and more naked would be the expression of this 'law', the more crude would be the forms assumed by this bureaucratism, and the more dangerous would it become for socialist development. The Soviet state is prevented not only from dying away, but even from freeing itself of the bureaucratic parasite... by... factors such as material want, cultural backwardness and the resulting dominance of the 'bourgeois law' in... the business of insuring... personal existence. (RB,55–6)

Trotsky did not respond to the idea that with the increasing complexity of social life and specialization there is an inexorable tendency to bureaucratization in most areas of social life, and that these tendencies might be exaggerated in a socialist state, particularly a backward state which must rely on bureaucratic organization to establish and organize its industries. He did not fully take account of the functional explanations of bureaucratization. He did not explain how complex administration could be non-bureaucratic. Trotsky argued, in short, that material inequality gave rise to social antagonisms, which necessitated a state. The state was perpetuated in its role of applying or enforcing the bourgeois law of distribution, which reproduced material inequality. As long as the Soviet Union had not broken out of its isolation, the 'ultra-bureaucratic' character of the state would remain. The ultimate solution to these problems lay with the world revolution, including the economic assistance it would bring, and the development of Russia's own productive forces. That is why Trotsky emphasized the importance of Soviet foreign policy.

Trotsky believed that a state and a bureaucracy existed because of the poverty of the transitional society. To this extent it was inevitable that they continued to exist, no matter whether Stalin or Trotsky led the Bolshevik Party:

The present Soviet society cannot get along without a state, nor even—*within limits* [my emphasis]—with a bureaucracy. But the cause of this is by no means the pitiful remnants of the past, but the mighty forces and tendencies of the present. The justification for the existence of a Soviet state as an apparatus of compulsion lies in the fact that the present transitional structure is still full of social contradictions, which in the sphere of *consumption*—most closely and sensitively felt—are extremely tense, and forever threaten to break over into the sphere of production. (RB,111–12)

If a state, and thus a bureaucracy, are to a certain extent inevitable after a socialist revolution, how would this privileged minority 'grow into' socialism? And to what *extent* are they necessary? Was Trotsky merely objecting to the size of the bureaucracy, to the proportion of the social surplus product which it devours, or to its political influence? Such a bureaucracy would have to be brought to socialism by the revolutionary party. He believed that the Bolshevik Party had discarded its responsibilities in favour of the material benefits it gained by joining the privileged minority it ought to have supervised. Trotsky objected to the bureaucracy having too much power, and imposing its rule over society: to a 'bureaucratic state of the Stalinist type'.

41

Whatever Trotsky had to say on the inevitability of a state and bureaucracy in a transitional regime, the 'degeneration' of the Party was another matter entirely. This point has not always been appreciated. As astute a commentator as John Plamenatz, for example, declared:

If Marxist theory is accepted, Trotsky's arguments seem good. But in that case the triumph of Stalin and all he stands for was inevitable. Of what use is it, then, to complain that the revolution was betrayed? [12]

That the building of socialism in Russia must proceed through a phase of bureaucratic rule is Deutscher's thesis, not Trotsky's. In the conditions of backwardness, political upheaval, and economic disintegration which accompanied Russia's effort in the First World War, and with a small urban working class and overwhelming peasantry, the Bolsheviks took charge of the state apparatus in the interests of the proletariat. Trotsky argued that the Party had succumbed to the pressures of its environment and 'degenerated', such that the bureaucracy now predominated. From guarding the proletariat's interests against the conflicting forces inherent in the existence of a state apparatus, the Party had begun to represent the interests of the bureaucracy.

How could a party of fine revolutionaries make this transformation? Trotsky implied that some of them, even in 1917, were not so fine and resolute, and that the prevalence of such types meant that the Party became subject to the influence of outside pressures. He also implied that many of the Old Bolsheviks were tempted by the privileges of power; he himself was made of stronger stuff. Not all Oppositionists were so endowed. Some, such as Adolf Joffe, committed suicide. In 1924, after the wrongful expulsion from the Party and subsequent suicide of Mikhail Glazman, one of Trotsky's secretaries, Trotsky scathingly attacked the Party leadership for persecuting genuine revolutionaries. After August 1918, he declared, Glazman 'became my closest collaborator'; Glazman's 'was the authority of moral strength, revolutionary duty, honesty, and supreme selflessness'. [13]
The Revolution Betrayed was written before the famous 'purge trials' of most of the remaining Old Bolshevik leaders in 1937–38. During these trials, Trotsky altered his arguments to support the view that Stalin had triumphed because he had eliminated the Old Guard, now represented implicitly as exemplars of Bolshevism. Things were not this clear, however, in 1935–36, and Trotsky thought that most of the Old Bolsheviks were guilty of moral turpitude.

Because the Party occupied such a central place in the new state, it was as a result of its degeneration that the bureaucracy had assumed unrivalled power. The bureaucracy had triumphed over the masses early in the 1920s, Trotsky argued in 1936 (RB,105). After much vacillation, discussed below, Trotsky decided that this was the meaning of the Soviet 'Thermidor' (TW 1934–35,166). The bureaucracy, far from being simply an arm of the new state, kept under close scrutiny by the Party, had now become supreme. The Party had become 'the political organisation of the bureaucracy' (RB,138).

The factors which increased the power of the bureaucracy were at the same time factors in the degeneration of the Party. Trotsky attributed their underlying cause to a reaction among the masses, venting itself through the Party as the only form of legal, political expression in the country.

Bolshevism... never identified itself either with the October Revolution or with the Soviet state that issued from it. Bolshevism considered itself as one of the factors of history, the 'conscious' factor—a very important but not decisive one.... Having taken over the state, the party is able, certainly, to influence the development of society with a power inaccessible to it before; but in return it submits itself to a ten time greater influence from all other elements of society. [14]

Rather than having just one party, subject to various pressures, and succumbing to the influence of alien classes, might it have been better (accepting this scenario) to have various parties each openly representing certain interests? The Bolshevik Party, Trotsky suggested (in a revised version of the notion that opposition views within the Party represented different class forces) became a political system in microcosm, and was not institutionally or morally equipped to cope.

The anti-revolutionary reaction among the masses, Trotsky volunteered, was caused by the deaths of large numbers of the best workers and Bolsheviks during the Civil War; by the masses' disappointment in the results of the Revolution; and by the Bolsheviks becoming removed from the masses. 'The new commanding caste rose to its place upon this wave' (RB,89). In fact, this sort of reaction or 'downswing' was formulated by Trotsky as a 'law' of revolution (RB,88; TW 1932,289). He had hoped that 'class conscious' workers, whom he tried to entice into the Party during the New Course period, would reinvigorate the leadership's commitment to the proletariat. The Lenin Levy did not dissuade him: the right type of member was not enrolled. Clashing with the 'petty-bourgeois opposition' in the American Trotskyist movement sixteen years later, Trotsky confidently forecast that

When a few thousand workers join the [Socialist Workers'] party, they will call the petty-bourgeois anarchists severely to order. The sooner, the better. (IDM,92)

He earnestly contrasted the 'instinctive' acceptance by the workers of dialectical materialism with the handicaps faced by 'bourgeois intellectuals' (IDM,86). In 1923, however, he had not appreciated the 'downswing' of revolution. Trotsky believed that social antagonisms were expressed through the Party (RB,98), and in this he found fundamental agreement with Stalin. Much of the rationale for purging the Party during the 1930s and '40s was founded on this common conception.

Trotsky distinguished between the existence of a state and a bureaucracy in a transitional regime, and the triumph of the bureaucracy over the Party and thus over the masses.

Out of social necessity there has developed an organ which has far outgrown its socially necessary function, and become an independent factor and therewith the source of great danger for the whole social organism. (RB,113)

Trotsky was aware of, and apparently endorsed, Rakovsky's 1929 distinction between a 'functional' and a 'social' bureaucracy (RB,102), a bureaucracy which functioned in the interests of the proletariat, and one which functioned in its own interests; but he did not use these terms. His discussion of the Stalinist bureaucracy clearly put it in the category of a social bureaucracy, a bureaucracy 'for itself', since the leaders of the Bolshevik Party had betrayed the ideals of the October Revolution to it. Trotsky thought it legitimate to use the notion of a conscious 'betrayal', because the degeneration of the Party was not inevitable. Trotsky argued that most of the Bolshevik *leaders* had been aware of the dangers of power: 'The very centre of Lenin's attention and that of his colleagues' he claimed, 'was occupied by a continual concern to protect the Bolshevik ranks from the vices of those in power' (RB,95). Had only the leaders the moral fortitude to 'protect' the ranks? And was the Bolshevik Party when in power really in power? To Trotsky it was apparent that to a 'vast degree the conquerors have assimilated the morals of the conquered' (RB,103).

The degeneration of the Bolshevik Party, according to Trotsky, occurred in stages. The early merging of Party and state had harmed the internal Party regime (although he neglected to mention his early advocacy of the incorporation of the trade unions into the state); the 'democratic' component of democratic centralism had begun to break down. In 1922, Lenin

was preparing a struggle against the faction of Stalin, which had made itself the axis of the party machine as a first step toward capturing the machinery of state. (RB,97)

Then the Party machine was freed from rank-and-file control through the Lenin Levy. T.H. Rigby attests to the use of these enrolments in the political campaigns of Stalin against his rivals for leadership, but not for the separation of leadership from Party control. [15] Trotsky summed up the process of degeneration as follows:

From the first days of the Soviet regime the counterweight to bureaucratism was the party. If the bureaucracy managed the state, still the party controlled the bureaucracy. Keenly vigilant lest inequality transcend the limits of what was necessary, the party was always in a state of open or disguised struggle with the bureaucracy. The historic role of Stalin's faction was to destroy this duplication, subjecting the party to its own officialdom and merging the latter in the officialdom of the state. Thus was created the present totalitarian regime. (RB,279)

Trotsky's objection to Soviet bureaucratization was not that more and more areas of social life were coming under the auspices of bureaucratic organization, but that the state bureaucracy had gained power over the Bolshevik Party. It was the power of the bureaucracy, and how it was acquired, which were at issue. But what of this ruling bureaucracy itself; what did Trotsky contribute to our understanding of it? Trotsky did not attempt a sociology of bureaucracy, or a comparative study of different types of bureaucracy, or even suggest alternatives to bureaucracy. He explained the role of the Stalinist bureaucracy, and the consequences of its rule, in political, not sociological, terms. Trotsky's use of the term 'bureaucracy' was rather broad. He identified bureaucracy in terms of its functions and its characteristics. Its members had a relatively high income, and thus formed a privileged social group, having access to goods and facilities not available to ordinary Russians (RB,102, 107, 115, 123). It had an administrative, and not a productive function (RB,135, 138), although considering that he believed it had a role in distribution (RB,59) it could indeed be said to have a productive function. It was a policeman and arbitrator, that is, it performed a necessary social role: 'Bureaucracy and social harmony are inversely proportional to one another' (RB,52). It was, he added, not necessarily homogeneous (RB,139). And, finally, it exercised political rule (RB,249). It is the last claim which is the source of most of the debate and confusion surrounding Trotsky's analysis.

Rather than defining bureaucracy as an organizational structure, with the office and its relations to other offices being more important than transitory incumbents, Trotsky concentrated on the social types which inhabited the structure. His argument lends itself to the view

45

that the structure encourages or produces certain social types. His continual coupling of privilege and bureaucracy also implies that a social bureaucracy is not just a structure but a social relation, an independent social power. He himself classified bureaucracy as a 'social category' (RB,136).

The logical starting point for analysing this social category is still, however, its organizational framework. Trotsky explained that the bureaucracy is the state's 'administrative apparatus' (RB,135). It consisted of the central state apparatus, including the military and naval departments as well as the secret police; the trade union, co-operative and 'other' general staffs; and interwoven with these, the staff of the Bolshevik Party. But these were only the 'dignitaries' of the bureaucracy. Below this level were the administrative pyramids of state, Party, trade unions, etc. The bureaucracy, according to Trotsky, also included the directors and vice-directors, administrative and technical personnel of industrial enterprises. This 'head count' included presidents and organizers of Soviet collective farms, and administrators and specialists in the Soviet economy. It even included the families of bureaucrats, although at what remove is unclear. All of these, Trotsky claimed, did 'not engage directly in productive labour' (RB,138). By 'productive labour' Trotsky did not intend to enter the debate over what is and is not 'productive' in terms of Marx's theory, (i.e., whether 'productive' connotes more than the creation of surplus value for capital). He simply meant that these people did not directly produce goods. Yet large-scale production requires more than those who make the goods; and if the market is not to allocate resources, there must also be planners. He concluded: 'Twelve percent, or perhaps 15 percent, of the population—that is the authentic social basis of the autocratic ruling circles' (RB,139). But to speak of a social basis is quite different from the *functional* basis of the bureaucracy he described. Certainly the families of bureaucrats benefited from their positions, but why should they form part of the bureaucracy? Trotsky did not confront the problems associated with transforming a functional into a social category.

The positions and categories Trotsky included in his survey of the bureaucracy are broad enough to encompass almost anyone in a particular functional role. But is there a bureaucracy, or are there many bureaucracies? Are the interests of all these bureaucrats identical, or are their functional interests (relating to their particular areas of concern) different from their overall social interests? If they have a unified social interest, how is it expressed? What is their ideology? And since position and status is the essence of bureaucracy,

46

how does their social unity overcome these internal (horizontal and vertical) differences? How, on top of all this, does the bureaucracy actually rule, and what does it mean to rule? If bureaucracy 'rules', then it would seem to rule by default of political leadership. What is the policy of the bureaucracy, and how is it decided? Can the bureaucracy decide on policy, or does it merely implement policy? As Ivan Szelenyi has pointed out, if bureaucrats are chiefly concerned with means, not ends, then it may be inappropriate to talk of a 'ruling bureaucracy' in the USSR:

the orthodox soviet Marxist view that under socialism bureaucracy does not exist makes sense in a way. The 'teleological redistributor' is basically of different social nature than Weber's bureaucrat.... Bureaucratic power properly defined can exist only in a world where techne dominates telos. [16]

Trotsky maintained that the bureaucracy viewed problems from the point of view of administration rather than politics. This notion was first advanced in 1923 and reinforced in subsequent years as he criticized Stalin's economic plans. In 1930 Trotsky even argued, rather fantastically, that 'administrative factors' were determining the wholesale collectivization and industrialization (TW 1930,107). *The Revolution Betrayed* echoed this theme, highlighting the 'administrative reflexes' with which the bureaucracy reacted to events (RB,62). Trotsky's alternative to a bureaucratic state of the Stalinist type was a 'strong state, but without mandarins' (RB,50). But are all bureaucrats 'mandarins'? Trotsky's descriptions conjure up many different and conflicting images.

To fit Stalin himself into this theoretical framework posed certain problems. After Lenin's death, Stalin towered over all events in Russia. He was no mere administrator, and had served many years apprenticeship in the Bolshevik Party in Tsarist times. In fact, Lenin in his so-called 'Testament' had cited Trotsky, not Stalin, as displaying an 'excessive preoccupation with the purely administrative side of the work'. [17] Trotsky denigrated Stalin's Bolshevism and his theoretical ability; this approach also suited his general appraisal and loathing of Stalin as a nonentity who had usurped power. He regarded Stalin as a pedestrian politician, whose key personal characteristics were 'love of power, ambition, [and] envy'. [18] Trotsky's uncompleted *Stalin* is riddled with personal innuendo and slurs. It is, as Knei-Paz relates, 'an exercise in demonology'. [19]

To explain how such a nonentity as Stalin rose to lead the bureaucracy and the Soviet state, Trotsky resorted to the notion that leaders were thrown up by the interests they represented, not by any outstanding personal characteristics:

The consecutive stages of the great French Revolution... demonstrate... that the strength of the 'leaders' and 'heroes' that replaced each other consisted primarily in their correspondence to the character of those classes and strata which supported them. (RB,87)

This is an approach quite at odds with his rather more sophisticated reading of literature and art in general, as being influenced by class society and its struggles, but as not being reducible to them. Because Trotsky could not attribute any worthwhile positive or imaginative traits to Stalin, he argued that Stalin personified the 'Thermidorian' bureaucracy:

Before he felt out his own course, the bureaucracy felt out Stalin himself. He brought it all the necessary guarantees: the prestige of an Old Bolshevik, a strong character, narrow vision, and close bonds with the political machine as the sole source of his influence. (RB,93)

Late in the 1930s, Trotsky claimed that Abel Yenukidze, a Georgian Bolshevik who fell from Stalin's favour in 1935, while not a careerist, was weak: 'Because of his whole character, Yenukidze could not escape being found in the camp of Thermidor'. [20] The socialist revolution, for Trotsky, put each to the test.

The affinity that Trotsky claimed existed between Stalin and the bureaucracy was one reason why he had earlier dismissed Stalin as a serious contender for leadership. In exile at Alma Ata, Trotsky characterized the Stalin faction as a 'centrist' current. [21] Since this faction was identified with the bureaucracy, as being buffeted on one side by the 'genuine revolutionaries' (Trotsky) who represented the workers, and on the other by the Right wing of the Party (Bukharin, Tomsky) who represented a transmission belt for *kulak* and bourgeois influences, [22] its tendency was described as 'bureaucratic centrism'. Trotsky explained 'centrism' as follows:

The two *fundamental* currents in the world working class are social imperialism [reformism] on the one hand and revolutionary communism on the other. Between these two poles come a number of *transitional* currents and groupings that are constantly changing... going sometimes from reformism to communism, sometimes from communism to reformism. These *centrist* currents do not have, and by their very nature cannot have, a well-defined social base. (TW 1930,236)

While communism was based on the working class, and reformism was based on the privileged sections of the working class, centrism had no clear social base. At this stage, Trotsky's analysis was fashioned to support two points: that the Bolshevik Party oscillated between reformism and communism, depending on the sorts of outside pres-

48

sures placed upon it, and could thus still be regenerated by sufficient proletarian pressure; and that the bureaucracy was not a stable social base (such as a social class), but a transient social formation without a policy of its own.

During the 1930s, this 'neither reformism, nor communism' approach to the policies of the Soviet bureaucracy (reminiscent of his costly 'neither war nor peace' stance at Brest Litovsk) gave way to a different interpretation based on a different model. In it, historical analogies with the French Revolution played a major role. 'Thermidor', in particular, was a concept which haunted the Bolsheviks from the mid-1920s. [23] In the month of Thermidor 1794, Robespierre was overthrown by more moderate elements within the Convention. Until 1935, Trotsky resisted the idea that Thermidor had occurred in the USSR, arguing that there had been no restoration of capitalism and no shift in power from one class to another (TW 1929,284). In 1935, however, he suddenly decided that Thermidor had occurred around 1923-24 (TW 1934-35,182). His new conception of Thermidor rested not upon the idea of a restoration of the old ruling class, but on how the spoils were divided among the victors. It was an essential prelude for his re-evaluation of the bureaucracy's role and social basis, which he called 'Bonapartism' (since the original Bonaparte had emerged after the original Thermidor). By this he meant a dictatorship based on the military, police and state bureaucracy; a regime with a certain independence from classes, but ultimately determined by them:

The Soviet bureaucracy—'Bolshevist' in its traditions but in reality having long since renounced its traditions, petty bourgeois in composition and spirit—was summoned to regulate the antagonism between the proletariat and peasantry, between the workers' state and world imperialism.... (TW 1934-35,180)

Whatever one might think of this characterization, and the historical analogy on which it was based, it underlines the fact that Trotsky did not see the bureaucracy as having power as an institution (as bureaucracy), but as a relation between classes. Trotsky continued to deny that the bureaucracy was a ruling class, and wrote:

Despite monstrous bureaucratic degeneration, the *Soviet state* still remains the historical instrument of the working class insofar as it assures the development of economy and culture on the basis of nationalized means of production and, by virtue of this, prepares the conditions for the genuine emancipation of the toilers through the liquidation of the bureaucracy and of social inequality. (TW 1934-35,170-1)

Trotsky defined the Soviet Union as a society transitional between capitalism and socialism (RB,47). This period was designated by Marx, and later endorsed by Lenin, as the 'dictatorship of the proletariat'. Trotsky, early in the life of the regime, called it a 'workers' state', by which he meant much the same thing. He seemed to take the idea of 'dictatorship' as a political form more literally than did Lenin, and the term 'workers' state' included not only the dictatorship of the proletariat but the economic base which Trotsky thought appropriate to the transition. In general, Trotsky was little disposed to discuss Marxist theory in any depth. Winston Churchill, in an otherwise hysterical discussion, perspicaciously remarked of him: 'It is probable that Trotsky never comprehended the Marxian creed: but of its drillbook he was the incomparable master'. [24] It was perhaps because of this that Trotsky had the ability to respond creatively to new situations, and not be bound by time-worn formulations.

For Trotsky, the workers' state had two crucial elements: its 'social content' and its 'political form'. The social content was actually its economic structure:

The nationalization of the land, the means of industrial production, transport, and exchange, together with the monopoly of foreign trade, constitute the basis of the Soviet social structure. (RB,248)

This definition makes a strict separation between economic base and political superstructure, essential and inessential. Thus he conceived of the political dictatorship of the bureaucracy on the social basis of the workers' state. Lenin suggested that proletarian dictatorships, like dictatorships of the bourgeoisie (by which he meant all capitalist countries), would be compatible with different types of political rule. Karl Kautsky had objected in 1925 that

The dictatorship of the proletariat is quite a different matter. It cannot arise from an economic or intellectual superiority which finds expression under all forms of government. It can only be the result of the possession of political power by the workers, which fact presupposes a definite form of government. [25]

Trotsky rejected this argument. But he assumed that the political form of the dictatorship of the proletariat was dedicated to the interests of the proletariat. This was now, in his own estimation, not the case. In 1935 he explained that 'The *social* domination of a class... may find extremely diverse *political* forms' (TW 1934–35,172); and 'the *social content of the dictatorship of the bureaucracy is determined by those productive relations that were created by the proletarian revolution*' (TW 1934–35,173). Marxists have often argued that the dictatorship of the bourgeoisie coexists with a number of different political forms, and Lenin claimed that the political dominance of the Bolsheviks ensured the dictatorship of the proletariat. But there are two other factors to consider. First, in Lenin's (and Trotsky's early) arguments, the proletarian *character* of the Bolshevik Party and its leadership was taken for granted. Second, to say that a social class is dominant is to say that that class derives some direct benefit from its position. This did not obtain under the rule of the Stalinist bureaucracy (nor earlier). Trotsky admitted only that the Stalinist state did not serve the proletariat. In 1928, it should be noted, Trotsky used another, political, definition of the workers' state, in which he insisted that nationalized property was a necessary, but not sufficient, criterion for defining a workers' state. [26] He soon abandoned this troublesome notion.

The writings of Marx on the subject of the 'dictatorship of the proletariat' are desultory and inconclusive, and those of Lenin are for the most part disingenuous. In the *Communist Manifesto*, for example, Marx declared that the transition to socialism would 'raise the proletariat to the position of ruling class' and 'win the battle of democracy'. [27] Elsewhere he spoke of an energetic dictatorship directed against the revolution's enemies. Lenin wrote in 1917:

Democracy for the vast majority of the people, and suppression by force, i.e., exclusion from democracy, of the exploiters and oppressors of the people—this is the change democracy undergoes during the *transition* from capitalism to Communism. [28]

When it suited him, Lenin used 'democracy' in a substantive, rather than in an institutional or formal sense. The rule of even one man— if he properly represented the interests of the proletariat, the 'vast majority'—was for Lenin more 'democratic' than even the most formally democratic of the 'bourgeois democracies'. The problem with his approach, which permeated Bolshevik ranks, was that there was no way of knowing, or at least testing, whether the Party or its leader(s) truly represented the proletariat.

The formal political structure of the Soviet republic did not figure large in Trotsky's calculations. Trotsky had as little respect for parliamentary democracy and the liberal freedoms associated with it as had Lenin. Rather, the issue for him was whether he or Stalin genuinely represented the interests of the proletariat. This did not prevent him from presenting the undemocratic, bureaucratic and highly repressive Soviet regime under Stalin to his own advantage in the West. Faced with a bureaucratic dictatorship which was repugnant to him, rather than with a Party dictatorship of the type he had helped to lead, Trotsky concluded that this workers' state was not of the 'usual' variety. The bureaucracy operated industry for its own benefits, yet the nationalized industry created by the 'proletarian'

51

revolution remained: here was a 'degenerated workers' state'. The political form was secondary to the economic foundation, even though Trotsky had earlier declared:

Politics is concentrated economics. At the present stage, the economic question in the Soviet republic more than ever is reduced to a question of politics. (TW 1929,122)

Even for Marxists, however, this separation of politics and economics is artificial. The political form of the transition gives meaning to the economic, and adds another dimension to the class struggle. [29] The Soviet state nationalized property in 1918, partly against its will, but nationalization means simply 'belonging to the state'. Ultimately, the character of the state must determine whether such nationalizations are a development towards socialism. Since the Bolshevik Party controlled the state, in Trotsky's perspective the nationalizations were indeed progressive developments. The Bolsheviks, however, no longer ruled, except in name. Did the 'social content' of the nationalizations thereby change when the bureaucracy took power? Mavrakis has written that 'In a country in which the state disposes of the means of production, the decisive question is to know who holds power'. [30]

Trotsky refused to abandon the Leninist heritage. He could not, therefore, appeal to formal means for authenticating the proletariat's representatives. Rather, he claimed that the Bolshevik Party had fundamentally altered, or 'degenerated'. His evidence—Soviet economic and foreign policy—was indirect and not compelling. And although he argued that the proletarian character of the state was guaranteed by the nationalized economy and state monopoly of foreign trade, both were political expedients of sorts. Nationalization was relaxed under NEP, and the Central Committee once even proposed to revoke the monopoly on certain goods, although they were opposed by Lenin and Trotsky, and eventually defeated. [31] To make his analysis coherent, Trotsky had to maintain the myth of the 'golden age' of Bolshevik rule in Russia under Lenin, when workers' democracy flourished and the 'achievements' of the October Revolution were consolidated. 'A victorious revolution' Trotsky wrote, is 'not only political institutions, but also a system of social relations' (RB,251–2). These social relations, according to him, had not yet been overthrown. The bureaucracy, he added, had 'expropriated the proletariat politically' (RB,249), but this is to assume that the proletariat once held political power. Trotsky meant that the bureaucracy had politically expropriated those sections of the Bolshevik Party which truly represented the proletariat.

In 1933, Trotsky explained that the functions of the bureaucracy 'relate basically to the *technique* of class rule. The existence of a bureaucracy... characterises *every* class regime' (TW 1933–34,112–13). He did not concede that the problems of bureaucracy might have particular importance for socialist or 'transitional' regimes because of the centralization of all life and economic activity, and because of the increasing complexity of all economic life. In *The Revolution Betrayed*, he claimed that 'the character of the economy as a whole... depends upon the character of the state power' (RB,250). But here, Trotsky's notion of the state as a historical class formation, rather than a formal structure of rule, turns what must be proved into an assumption.

For Trotsky, the Soviet bureaucracy was unique in its independence: 'In no other regime has a bureaucracy ever achieved such a degree of independence from the dominating (sic) class' (RB,248). It was unique in its 'bourgeois customs' (RB,249), and in its control over the nation's riches (RB,249). The bureaucracy had supreme political, and thus economic, control. He therefore declared:

we cannot deny that it is *something more* than a bureaucracy. It is in the full sense of the word the sole privileged and commanding stratum in the Soviet society. (RB,249. Emphasis added.)

Trotsky was adamant, however, that the Soviet bureaucracy was not a new ruling class. At the base of the Soviet state, he claimed, lay the basis for socialism; the bureaucracy had not yet succeeded in destroying this base and substituting its own property relations.

Classes, Trotsky argued, are characterized 'primarily by their relation to the means of production' (RB,248). Thus in capitalist society, the bourgeoisie owns the means of production and the proletariat does not. But it could be argued that since the state 'belongs' to the bureaucracy (RB,249) [32], and the means of production belong to the state, then the means of production 'belong' to the bureaucracy. This formulation ignores the distinction between ownership and control, although Trotsky took the fact that the bureaucracy could not legally 'own' property in the USSR as decisive. Ownership and control, as Berle and Means first argued in 1932, [33] are becoming more and more distinct in modern societies. James Burnham later took up this theme in his *The Managerial Revolution*, arguing that a ruling class was one which controlled the means of production, but did not necessarily own them. Trotsky, however, insisted that 'property relations are validated by laws' (RB,248), and that if the bureaucracy were a class, it would 'own' the means of production, its proprietorial rights being codified in the Constitution. [34] Trotsky's definition of social class is fundamentally juridical. Ironically, in capitalist societies the class which owns the means of production, but has little to do directly with political rule, is here considered a 'ruling class'; yet the Soviet elite which is demarcated sufficiently by the system of *nomenklatura*, has ultimate control of the means of production and clearly participates in ruling institutions, is not. Perhaps our 'inherited labels', and particularly the Marxist shibboleth 'ruling class', are inappropriate for analysing the Soviet social structure, as Alec Nove has recently suggested. [35] Perhaps such labels are altogether inappropriate; before we start splitting hairs, we ought to make sure that we are on the right head.

Trotsky added that a bureaucrat cannot bequeath to his heirs his position in the bureaucracy. However, because knowledge is still central to Soviet bureaucracies, the bureaucrat's privileges and money can assure the best education for his children and can thus almost guarantee them a future in the elite. Elites have always worked in this way, which is not to say that people of ability from any stratum will not be recruited into them. [36] To assert that the bureaucracy is a ruling class, Trotsky suggested, is to say that it *exploits* the proletariat. Therefore, he ingeniously distinguished between exploitation and 'parasitism'. The latter concept, lacking precise economic definition, was proposed a couple of years before *The Revolution Betrayed*:

To put it plainly, insofar as the bureaucracy robs the people... we have to deal not with *class exploitation*... but with *social parasitism*. (TW 1933-34,114)

While he was careful not to attribute 'ownership' to Soviet bureaucrats, he accused them of 'robbing' the proletariat—itself a juridical notion. Trotsky argued that in so far as the bureaucracy squandered a huge proportion of the national wealth on itself, it did so on the basis of the 'social relations' established by the October Revolution. The squandering depended on the new social relations, which he believed were characteristic of a workers' state. Does the American clergy constitute a special ruling class, Trotsky asked rhetorically? No, he declared. But does it not devour a large proportion of surplus value? Even so, it is not a ruling class (although Trotsky neglected the fact that it was not involved in governing and had no pretension to govern). Trotsky illustrated his point with another analogy. Trade union bureaucrats might be compared with Soviet bureaucrats as parasites on the organized workers' movement: 'In the last analysis a workers' state is a trade union which has conquered power' (IDM,25). At the basis of these arguments is an assumption which Trotsky does not examine: that exploitation only operates between

54

social classes.

Trotsky's analysis depended on the idea that new 'social relations' were established by the October Revolution, that these social relations were based on and appropriate to nationalized property, and that the bureaucracy arose within them, and had not destroyed them. Trotsky's language on this basic point is not consistent, and the Marxist credentials of his argument are problematic. Marx, outlining the materialist conception of history in the 1859 Preface to *A Contribution to the Critique of Political Economy*, explained that 'the anatomy of civil society is to be sought in political economy'. [37] In producing their lives, he argued, men enter into definite relations of production, independent of their will, which constitute 'the economic structure of society', the foundation. On this base arises a 'legal and political superstructure'. The relations of production are expressed legally as property relations. Marx used this analysis of society to explain history, which he saw as the immanent development of society. History consists of the inexorable development of the productive forces at first being assisted by the relations of production (or property relations), but then being hindered by them. These restraints are eventually destroyed, and new relations of production come into being. In other words, certain relations of production (say, between capitalist and worker) correspond to certain property relations (private property): they are different aspects of the same social reality.

Now whatever we might think of Marx's schema of historical explanation, about its intellectual coherence or its adequacy to explain historical change, there is no doubt that Trotsky formally accepted it. The basis of Trotsky's entire argument rests on the claim that the October Revolution established socialist relations of production—or socialist property relations. In *The Revolution Betrayed*, for example, he declared that 'the social revolution... still exists in property relations' (RB,355). Legally, private property in the means of production did not exist in the USSR. So for Trotsky, socialist relations of production (which for Marx 'correspond to a definite stage of development of... material productive forces' [38]) had in fact preceded the appropriate material productive forces. The basic problem in the Soviet Union, therefore, was this lack of correspondence: 'the October Revolution produced... a contradiction between low national productive forces and socialist forms of property' (RB,300). The two had to be synchronized by expanding the productive forces.

Trotsky regarded Soviet nationalization as a socialist form of property, designating socialist relations of production. This strict correspondence between relations of production and forms of property

55

was not matched in his work by a similar correspondence between productive forces and relations of production. There was nothing imaginative about his use of these Marxist categories. His only real contribution in this field had been earlier, when he argued that where on a world scale there was a contradiction between capitalist relations of production and advanced productive forces backward countries had the chance to leap ahead to socialism. His analysis at this level, furthermore, suggested that bureaucratization was inevitable. In the 1920s he advocated rapid economic development so that the economic basis of the bureaucracy's existence would be undermined, but in the 1930s, with industrialization underway, he turned his attention more to the international expansion of revolution, and thus to Stalin's foreign policy. If he could not continue to maintain that the rulers protected their interests by obstructing industrialization, he could at least claim that an anti-revolutionary foreign policy maintained the bureaucracy in power. Economic development had, in fact, intensified bureaucratization.

The economic advances of the first Five-Year Plan (1929–1933) should, according to Trotsky's formula, have hastened a decrease in privilege. In reality, Trotsky conceded,

the opposite thing has happened: the growth of the productive forces has so far been accompanied by an extreme development of all forms of inequality, privilege and advantage, and therewith of bureaucratism. (RB,112)

But he still believed that economic development would ultimately reduce bureaucracy. During the first period of the Soviet regime, he explained, 'an equality of general poverty' (RB,112) reigned. Recent economic successes meant that now it was possible to give a good living only to a few:

The present state of production is still far from guaranteeing all necessities to everybody. But it is already adequate to give significant privileges to a minority, and convert inequality into a whip for the spurring on of the majority. (RB,112–13)

Wants, however, may be insatiable, and there was no guarantee that further development of the Soviet productive forces would not simply increase the privileges of the Soviet bureaucracy, even if it provided everybody with necessities. This holds particularly since Trotsky believed that the bureaucracy protected inequality, and that 'We cannot count on the bureaucracy's peacefully and voluntarily renouncing itself in behalf of socialist equality' (RB,253–4). Such a bureaucracy can be removed only through revolution: a 'political' revolution, Trotsky cautioned, and one which did not change the 'social conquests' of the October Revolution. On the road to socialism, he declared, 'the workers would have to overthrow the bureaucracy' (RB,255). The Soviet bureaucracy was well entrenched; it even, said Trotsky, had 'the specific consciousness of a ruling "class" which, however, is still far from confident of its right to rule' (RB,135).

The ultimate cause of the bureaucracy's ascendancy to power, according to Trotsky, was the 'dilatoriness of the world proletariat in solving the problems set for it by history' (RB,278). If the international revolution failed, he asserted, then a bourgeois counter-revolution in the USSR was likely (RB,290). In his *Transitional Program*, the founding programmatic document of the Fourth International, Trotsky wrote that unless it was crushed by the working class, the Soviet bureaucracy would become 'ever more the organ of the world bourgeoisie in the workers' state', and from it would come plans to 'overthrow the new forms of property and plunge the country back to capitalism'. [39] It is arguable that the 'social relations' created by October were somehow disagreeable to the bureaucracy. To concentrate on the failure of the international revolution, and the economic backwardness of Russia to explain the growth in power of the Soviet bureaucracy, as Trotsky did in *The Revolution Betrayed*, may seem plausible, but his real point was an indirect one. The factors he mentioned were really for him only crucial in relation to the 'degeneration' of the Bolshevik Party. If proletarian pressure, from inside or outside the USSR had been kept on the Party, its degeneration, and the betrayal of proletarian ideals by its leaders, would not have occurred. While Trotsky suggested reasons for bureaucratization, he believed that if the Bolshevik Party had retained its ideals the Soviet bureaucracy would have remained a servant of the proletariat. How long genuine Bolshevism could have survived alone in a hostile international environment he did not conjecture.

5

BOLSHEVISM REAFFIRMED

Less than two weeks after having completed *The Revolution Betrayed*, Trotsky learnt of the first of the 'Moscow Trials', in which most of the remaining Old Bolshevik leaders were to perish. But it was Trotsky and the son who acted as his lieutenant, Leon Sedov, who emerged as the chief defendants *in absentia*, allegedly directing a conspiracy to overthrow the Soviet regime. The murder of Politburo member, Kirov, in 1934 (then used as a pretext for a purge of Stalin's enemies [1]), was attributed to Zinoviev, Kamenev and others, acting on orders from Trotsky. It was the only murder for which they were charged. The chief prosecutor, Vyshinsky, declared: 'I demand that dogs gone mad should be shot, every one of them'. [2] They were sentenced to death on 24 August 1936.

It is now widely accepted in the West that the Soviet purge trials were based on trumped-up charges and falsified evidence, and were the culmination of a political campaign by Stalin to remove anyone who might threaten his position within the Party and the regime. This was not widely recognized at the time. To their discredit, many Western intellectuals rationalized and defended these outrageous trials. [3] Trotsky, having moved from Turkey to France and thence to Norway, was there placed under house arrest and his writings censored when he tried to reply to the charges against him. [4] He was relieved to find refuge in Mexico in January 1937, the month of the Second Moscow Trial. Denying Stalin's charge that he was an agent of fascism, Trotsky pledged that if he were found guilty of the charges by an independent commission of inquiry, he would place himself 'voluntarily in the hands of the executioners of the GPU'. [5] Such a commission began hearings in April that year, with John Dewey presiding. In December, Trotsky and his son were found not guilty. [6] Inside the USSR, the purges and 'judicial murder' continued. Red Army officers were purged; the Third, and last, Moscow Trial was held early in 1938. Bukharin and many others were sentenced to death for treason, espionage, sabotage, etc. [7]

Since 1933, Trotsky's life had been bound up with the creation of a Fourth International, his proposed international Leninist party.

In 1935 he wrote that his activity for a new International was 'the most important work of my life—more important than 1917, more important than the period of the Civil War, or any other.... [N]ow my work is "indispensable" in the full sense of the word'. [8] But the origins of the Fourth International were not auspicious, and it has been racked by disputes and splits. During the 1930s, small Trotskyist groups were expelled from Communist Parties, and remained isolated. Trotsky called on 'centrist' and independent revolutionary parties to join in the formation of the Fourth International. Few responded (TW 1933–34,49). Trotsky then counselled his followers to enter Social Democratic and other left-wing parties in order to influence their ranks and recruit new members. In 1934, for example, the French section of the International Communist League entered the French Socialist Party; in the United States, the Trotskyists entered, and destroyed, the Socialist Party. The 'Russian section' was represented at Trotskyist conferences by exiles, who had lost contact with their colleagues in the Soviet Union as early as 1932. [9] Isolated in labour camps, they probably knew nothing of the attempts to found the Fourth International. But long after their most outstanding local leaders had capitulated or been killed, many held out. One such group, eventually massacred in 1938, was recalled with some respect by an eyewitness at the Vorkuta mines, above the Arctic Circle. [10] Soviet agents killed a number of prominent Trotskyists in the West during the 1930s, probably including Leon Sedov, who died in mysterious circumstances in February 1938 in a Paris hospital after a routine operation. A 'river of blood', Trotsky declared, separated him from Stalin.

The founding conference of the Fourth International took place in September 1938, despite the opposition of the Polish delegation which included Isaac Deutscher. [11] The looming Second World War occasioned an even more serious controversy. For some Trotskyists, the Soviet invasion of Finland gave the lie to Trotsky's interpretation of the nature of the Soviet regime, and absolved revolutionaries from defending either. Trotsky himself soon suggested that the outcome of the War would be a decisive test for his interpretation (IDM,8–9;14). James Burnham, a Professor of Philosophy at New York University and an American Trotskyist, had as early as 1937 questioned Trotsky's analysis of the USSR as a degenerated workers' state. [12] On 22 August 1939, the day of the Stalin-Hitler pact, Burnham and Max Shachtman moved to have the question of the nature of the USSR discussed among the leaders of the Socialist Workers' Party. Burnham declared that 'It is impossible to regard the Soviet Union as a workers' state in any sense whatever'. [13] He believed that the Soviet Union's ruling bureaucracy constituted a definite social class, and dominated a 'bureaucratic collectivist' state. [14]

Burnham's thesis was not new. Indeed, only a few months before Burnham's dissent, Trotsky faced similar criticism from an ex-Trotskyist, Bruno Rizzi, author of *La Bureaucratisation du Monde*. [15] Trotskyism often faced this sort of challenge. John Wright, an American Trotskyist, related:

Beginning with 1930 a whole series of splits occurred over the constantly recurring differences relating to the class nature of the Soviet Union. If in 1939–40 this issue precipitated the struggle inside the Socialist Workers Party, then in 1930, at the very inception of the European movement, it led to a break with [Hugo] Urbahns in Germany, [Robert] Louzon in France, [Edouard Van] Overstraaten in Belgium, etc. [16]

Even at the founding conference of the Fourth International, a 'new class' thesis was advanced by Yvan Craipeau, a French delegate. [17]

Trotsky recognized that the future of Trotskyism as a distinct current in the Marxist movement was at stake in the dispute with Burnham. His first contribution to the debate defended his analysis of the 'class nature' of the Soviet Union, but the struggle soon became much broader. It was waged over three major areas: the 'Russian question'; the question of dialectics, which Trotsky considered both the core of Marxism and the source of the opposition's errors; and the 'organization question'. James P. Cannon, the leader of the majority in the Socialist Workers' Party, argued that the Burnham-Shachtman group was unified not on the 'Russian question', but on their desire to oust the Cannon regime. [18] After the initial stages of the discussion, the Russian question was almost entirely replaced by the question of dialectical method. There was nothing fundamental for Trotsky to add to his characterization of the Soviet regime, maintained since October 1933, that would convince his opponents. The Stalin-Hitler pact, on which they placed so great a store, revealed according to Trotsky merely the *extent* of the degeneration of the Bolshevik Party.

The terminological differences which separated the two groups were not vital; Trotsky himself conceded the tentative nature of his own formulations. 'It would... be a piece of monstrous nonsense to split with comrades who on the question of the sociological nature of the USSR have an opinion different from ours, insofar as they solidarize with us in regard to the political tasks' (IDM,5). But the differences proved deeper than terminology, and Trotsky restated his case for defending the workers' state. The major weakness of the opposition's position, as Trotsky recognized, was that they accepted the basis of his analysis:

Our critics as a rule take the facts as we long ago established them. They add absolutely nothing essential to the appraisal either of the position of the bureaucracy and the toilers, or of the role of the Kremlin on the international arena. In all these spheres, not only do they fail to challenge our analysis, but on the contrary they base themselves completely upon it and even restrict themselves to it. (IDM,4)

Trotsky felt no need to deepen or fundamentally reappraise the analysis of *The Revolution Betrayed*. The onus fell to the opposition to prove that some decisive change had occurred in the USSR to justify a change of characterization, since they did not challenge the operative criteria. Cannon was characteristically blunt: 'Has the economic structure of the Soviet Union' he asked, 'undergone a profound change since our party convention two months ago?' [19]

A correct position on the USSR, Trotsky lectured, was based on asking the right questions. They were:

(1) What is the historical origin of the USSR? (2) What changes has this state suffered during its existence? (3) Did these changes pass from the quantitative stage to the qualitative? That is, did they create a historically necessary domination by a new exploiting class? (IDM,52)

Trotsky's position was based on the (dubious) assumption that the USSR had been a 'workers' state' under the rule of the (genuine) Bolshevik Party. This assumption was not questioned during the debate. Clearly, Trotsky operated from a particular conception of history. For him to argue that the bureaucracy was a 'class' would signify that it was not merely a temporary growth on the workers' state, but a stable social form. History, Trotsky implied, would vindicate him. But this argument relies on a variable that is imponderable. Trotsky stressed such terms as 'transitory' and 'unstable', but all regimes and states are transitory in the scales of history. It was not actually the *form* of the present Soviet bureaucracy which worried Trotsky so much as the idea that it might endure. What length of time would it have taken for him to consider that the bureaucracy had become a class, that 'transitory' had become 'stable'?

To introduce his conception of history , Trotsky turned the debate to the question of dialectics. To be a class in the Marxist sense, Trotsky insisted innovatively, was to be 'historically necessary'. The Stalin regime was but a temporary phase: 'The Soviet oligarchy possesses all the vices of the old ruling classes but lacks their historical mission' (IDM,7). The Second World War, he believed, held the key to the future of society, and would confirm his notion of history.

The second world war has begun. It attests incontrovertibly to the fact that society can no longer live on the basis of capitalism. Thereby it subjects the proletariat to a new and perhaps decisive test. (IDM,8)

Trotsky hedged his bets, but he believed that the War would result in revolution, as the First World War had before it. Thus would the Soviet state cleanse itself of the bureaucracy's rule, and it would become apparent that 'the Soviet bureaucracy was only an *episodic* relapse' (IDM,9). This reliance on the validity of what he regarded as historical materialism was a new feature of Trotsky's analysis. Yet there was little else he could do to convince those who accepted so much of his original argument. History, he believed, moved in such a way as to compel the proletariat to take certain actions; history would spur them on.

For Trotsky, society was moving to a higher, socialist stage. The October Revolution was a giant step in that direction. As long as he considered that capitalism had not been restored in the USSR, the Soviet state remained in transition to socialism, no matter what one chose to name it. It did not represent a reversal of history, or a new direction in history. If his opponents did not accept his reasoning, then what were the alternatives? To Trotsky they seemed obvious:

Either the Stalin regime is an abhorrent relapse in the process of transforming bourgeois society into a socialist society, or the Stalin regime is the first stage of a new exploiting society.... However onerous the second perspective may be, if the world proletariat should actually prove incapable of fulfilling this mission placed upon it by the course of development, nothing else would remain except only to recognize that the socialist program, based on the internal contradictions of capitalist society, ended as a Utopia. (IDM,9)

It is interesting that Trotsky could theoretically conceive of this second possibility. He speculated that the proletariat may not be able to fulfil its 'historic tasks' as outlined by historical materialism. But he did not doubt the correctness of the Marxist analysis of capitalism: it would destroy itself by virtue of its 'internal contradictions'. Trotsky looked half-seriously at the post-capitalist options, only to dismiss those not sanctioned by Marx. Could the proletariat take up its responsibilities? Could it come to the aid of the revolutionary party that had taken power in its name? If it could not, then degeneration of any such party was inevitable.

Trotsky resorted to historical materialism to convince his opponents of the correctness of his analysis, yet he raised the possibility that historical materialism may be mistaken in its estimate of the proletariat. To convinced Marxists, Trotsky's appeal to historical materialism should have ended the debate; instead, Trotsky sowed the seeds of further doubt. In conjunction with this argument, Trotsky revealed that his commitment to socialism was based primarily on moral considerations. If a new society was created which was not included in the traditional Marxist schema, he stated, 'it is self-evident (sic) that a new "minimum" program would be required—for the defense of the interests of the slaves of the totalitarian bureaucratic society' (IDM,9). In other words, the historically necessary may not be the morally right.

In April 1940, Burnham and Shachtman quitted the Fourth International. Its International Executive Committee was immobilized, since most of its members had supported their line. An emergency International Conference was held in May 1940 to re-establish a functioning leadership. Trotsky was assassinated on 20 August. In 1938 he had predicted that the programme of the Fourth International 'will become the guide of millions and these revolutionary millions will know how to storm earth and heaven'. [20] Riven by disputes, deprived of its founder, and constantly troubled by the 'degenerated workers' state' thesis, the Fourth International has not fulfilled his expectations. Indeed, his theoretical legacy is its chief problem.

6

CONCLUSION

Trotsky was not the only critic of the Stalin regime, nor was he alone in emphasizing bureaucratization as one of its central features. Yet he approached the question of the nature of the regime from a distinct perspective. He was first of all a Marxist, with a faith in the future of mankind which is rare today, even for Marxists. He was also a Leninist, who (perhaps a little grudgingly) represented Lenin as the authentic voice of twentieth-century Marxism. He was, furthermore, one of the chief architects of the Bolshevik coup, and was attached to the glorious days of the Revolution and Bolshevik power. It is therefore not surprising that he rejected the idea that the USSR was a new form of capitalist, or exploitative, society, and that he would not accept that the bureaucracy was a new ruling class. Nor would he countenance the idea that the Soviet outcome was inherent in one-party rule. His was the Leninist alternative to Stalin. His position is all the more unusual if we consider his earlier status in the inner councils of the Party, and the consistency of his critique throughout the years of his opposition to Stalin's rule.

Trotsky in opposition claimed to be a democrat and a Leninist. But democratic Leninism, which he contrasted to the supposed anti-Leninism of Stalin, is democratic only by virtue of being proletarian, and is proletarian by means no democrat would recognize. Trotsky believed that the Bolshevik Party and even its leader alone could properly represent the historical interests of the proletariat. His concessions to Soviet democracy (for he was fond of the idea of soviets), were designed to permit proletarian moral pressure to be applied to the Bolsheviks, not to generate alternative governments. Yet how, in his own terms, could a (genuine) working class party be opposed to (genuine) Bolshevism? What he advocated in opposition would have been anathema to him in power—and, he would have reasoned, unnecessary. Trotsky never invoked formal democracy as a means of getting his viewpoint heard in the Party or the Soviet Union. For him, it was a matter of internal proletarian opposition (spurning the traditions of 'bourgeois democracy'), forced into open struggle against erstwhile colleagues, but never appealing to the class enemy or his institutions. Trotsky defiantly insisted that the post-Lenin leaders of the Party were traitors to Bolshevism.

But there are good reasons for doubting that Trotsky's was a thoroughgoing alternative to Stalin's rule. His campaign against bureaucratization, for example, was a demand not for democracy, but to 'restore' the Party's proletarian character. It is generally assumed that when Trotsky joined the Party he abandoned his analysis of Leninism as 'substitutionism'. But although he did not revive the analysis, and although his followers are loath to translate and republish it, he never renounced it. Instead, he re-evaluated 'substitutionism' as being not intrinsically pernicious. Properly to represent the working class, and effectually to substitute for it, depended on the qualities of the aspiring substitutes. In 1917, Trotsky believed that the Bolsheviks had earned the right to substitute themselves for the proletariat. Thereafter, he stressed those characteristics which had merited their historical role; indeed, he came to identify certain traits as being fundamental to Bolshevism. Thus his assessment of the moral qualities of the Bolsheviks was essential to his analysis of the Soviet regime. Not the institutions, but the revolutionary personnel guaranteed the transition to socialism. As a Bolshevik, Trotsky accepted the logic of substitutionism. He did not flinch from the conclusion that one man could embody the dictatorship of the proletariat, *provided that he was a man of impeccable character*, a genuine Bolshevik.

The regime had degenerated, he held, because many in the Party had sacrificed revolutionary goals to personal advancement. In 1923, Trotsky sought to rehabilitate the Party's leaders; he soon resolved to replace them. He offered the Bolsheviks moral fibre and admonition, when what they needed most was recuperation. He urged them to make ever greater sacrifices. Yet his view of the early years of Bolshevik rule was overly sanguine: the measures then taken were designed more to insure survival than to satisfy programmatic purity. Nevertheless, to these moves were soon assigned class labels. Those which received majority support among the leaders generally became 'proletarian'; losers became class enemies. In this respect, Leninism came to haunt Lenin's successors.

The isolation of the Soviet regime formed the backdrop to Trotsky's explanation of its degeneration. Trotsky (and, he claimed, Lenin) stressed that the Revolution would perish unless other successful socialist revolutions came to its aid. He argued that the bungling of international revolution under Stalin's leadership would not have occurred had the Comintern followed his prescriptions. Despite his disclaimers, Trotsky's estimation of the Comintern was similar to Stalin's; having the 'correct' line made all the difference. Trotsky relied on the *non sequitur* that Stalin's failures confirmed his own correctness. He could not risk considering that various revolutionary enterprises were doomed, whatever their leadership, for fear of confronting the issue of how Trotsky as *Vozhd* would have come to terms with the regime's isolation. Would tenacity have been enough to preserve Bolshevism until help arrived? Trotsky's conduct in exile added weight to his case against Stalinism. Irving Howe recalled: 'To have come even briefly under his influence during the 1930s was to learn a lesson in moral courage'. [1] But he was, after all, in exile.

Trotsky's analysis of the Soviet bureaucracy was subordinated to his defence of the surviving 'achievements' of the October Revolution. Before he considered the role, composition and significance of the bureaucracy, he pronounced that it was not a social class in Marx's sense. As a Marxist, Trotsky had a refreshing approach to novel situations; yet he was ultimately dogmatic. He could not conceive that the legal forms of nationalized property might be peculiar to a new form of class society, or give rise to a new form of exploitation. The sociological formulations which he employed to describe the bureaucracy, such as 'caste' and 'stratum', were at times recognized even by him as inadequate. But he assiduously avoided calling it a 'class'. His confession that the Soviet bureaucracy was 'something more' than a bureaucracy suggests that Marxist tools of social analysis may be inadequate to explain Soviet society. There are difficulties also in sustaining the traditional sense of the term 'bureaucracy'. The role of the Soviet bureaucracy, as Trotsky portrayed it, took it beyond established definitions. It was a group which set goals, as well as evaluating and carrying out the tasks for achieving those goals. In this respect, Trotsky made an interesting distinction between administrators and bureaucrats. In 1937, he explained that bureaucrats were 'demi-gods', while administrators were merely 'functionaries'. [2] What we might call 'bureaucrats', then, Trotsky labelled administrators. Trotsky's 'bureaucracy' is not a servant, but a new master. It is not even a servant which has come to dominate the master, but one which has replaced him. Trotsky and others have made a point of distinguishing between politics and administration. Accepting this distinction, a 'ruling bureaucracy' which must, of necessity, make governmental decisions, is a contradiction *in adjecto*.

If there are difficulties with Trotsky's analysis of the bureaucracy (especially on questions of its coherence, its ideology, and its separation from mere administration), it may have been that Trotsky was compelled to pursue the theme of bureaucratization, since it was an avenue for criticizing the regime which had the imprimatur of Lenin himself. But Trotsky's primary concern was with the revival of Bolshevism in Russia. Having linked the bureaucratization thesis with his moral critique of the Party leadership, he had to follow it through. Indeed, Trotsky suggested that bureaucratic modes of thought and behaviour paved the way for the transformation of the Party from an instrument of the proletariat into an arm of the bureaucracy.

From the Trotskyist movement has come a profusion of 'bureaucratic state' theories, to account for states as diverse as the USSR, Nazi Germany, and New Deal USA. They all trade upon the fact that the modern state and its bureaucracies administer ever larger areas of social life and are growing in extent and power. They trade also upon the difficulties that all of us experience, in one way or another, when dealing with bureaucracies. Bureaucracies arose to cope with phenomena which exhibit regularities, and on the whole they do this efficiently and well. Complaints about bureaucracy relate chiefly to exceptions, and arise because we value our individuality as the stereotyping momentum of bureaucratic procedure does not. But just as we often think of bureaucracies as juggernauts, advancing inexorably, almost out of control, how can we say that a bureaucracy 'rules'? A bureaucracy rules only by default; it generally does not initiate new directions. Governments are inevitably bound up with bureaucracies; but they are also concerned with leadership and direction. Theories of a bureaucratic society, if they are to be any more than observations about the growth in the power and size of bureaucracies in the modern world, seem to ignore or avoid the question of who rules, of who has the decisive say in government. They raise the possibility that, strictly speaking, no one rules. This, however, is probably more true of Western than other nations. Trotsky, it is clear, did not want to grant that Stalin ruled or made vital decisions about the direction of policy which Soviet bureaucracies put into effect. He claimed that Stalin was a mere figurehead. Yet even if bureaucrats from the highest departmental head to the lowliest clerk had the same interests *qua* bureaucrats, is the bureaucracy not internally divided, and are relations between bureaucrats not strictly regulated by position?

Trotsky's notion of the degenerated workers' state, the fruit of his analysis of Soviet bureaucratization, is unconvincing in two crucial respects. First, it is based on a cursory understanding of bureaucracy and its role. Secondly, it serves to disguise his moral outlook, and the importance of the moral standards he demanded from the revolutionary vanguard. Trotsky's 'remedies' for bureaucratization: intensifying industrialization, expanding the Party and furthering world socialist revolution were not really remedies for bureaucracy, but the means by which he hoped to rectify the moral malaise within the Party. Trotsky was not a democrat or a profound Marxist or other theorist, but a moralist.

NOTES

I. INTRODUCTION

1 Isaac Deutscher, *The Prophet Armed*, p. 258.
2 Baruch Knei-Paz, *The Social and Political Thought of Leon Trotsky*, especially Chapter 5.
3 Robert V. Daniels, *The Conscience of the Revolution*, pp. 63-9.
4 George Orwell, 'Politics and the English Language', *The Collected Essays, Journalism and Letters of George Orwell*, Vol. 4, p. 165. Of course, this quotation is capable of redounding upon the user!
5 Cited Irving Howe, *Trotsky*, p. 146.
6 See John Dewey, 'Means and Ends', in Trotsky, *Their Morals and Ours*, especially pp. 52-3.
7 Knei-Paz, p. 565: 'The problem... was not that Stalin used terror, violence, lies and calumny but that these instruments were utilized for non-socialist purposes and, *on this basis*, were rendered immoral'.
8 See Israel Getzler, *Kronstadt 1917-1921*, especially Chapter 6. Getzler refutes Trotsky's persistent assertions that the Kronstadters of 1921 were not those revolutionary sailors who had been crucial to Bolshevik victory in 1917.
9 Trotsky, *Terrorism and Communism*, p. 109; cf. Lenin, 'The Immediate Tasks of the Soviet Government', *Collected Works*, Vol. 27, p. 268.
10 Cited Deutscher, *The Prophet Armed*, p. 287.
11 Trotsky, *Stalin*, Vol. 2, p. 248.
12 *New Left Review*, No. 139, May-June 1983, p. 1.
13 Trotsky, *The Transitional Program for Socialist Revolution*, p. 72.
14 Howe, p. 163; Knei-Paz, pp. 23 and 512.
15 David W. Lovell, *From Marx to Lenin*, especially Chapter 2.
16 Joseph Hansen and William F. Warde, 'Introduction' to Trotsky, *In Defense of Marxism*, p. ix.

2. BOLSHEVISM BESIEGED

1 See Lenin, *Collected Works*, Vol. 26, p. 84, and E.H. Carr, *The Bolshevik Revolution*, Vol. 1, p. 104.

2 Deutscher, *The Prophet Armed*, p. 390.

3 See Deutscher, *The Prophet Unarmed*, pp. 86-7.

4 Ibid., p. 32.

5 Carr, *The Interregnum 1923-1924*, p. 309n.

6 On Trotsky's ill-health and its effects, see Daniels, pp. 226-7, and Deutscher, *The Prophet Unarmed*, p. 132n.

7 Carr, *The Interregnum*, p. 329.

8 See ibid., p. 340; Deutscher, *The Prophet Unarmed*, p. 125; and Daniels, p. 228.

9 Cited Carr, p. 346. Trotsky replied to this charge: see *The Challenge of the Left Opposition*, pp. 84 and 146.

10 Lenin, *'Left-Wing' Communism—An Infantile Disorder, Selected Works*, Vol. 3, p. 315.

11 Max Eastman, *Since Lenin Died*, pp. 80-1.

12 Deutscher, *The Prophet Unarmed*, p. 119.

13 Trotsky, *Problems of Everyday Life*, p. 51.

14 Cited Daniels, p. 221.

15 See Deutscher, *The Prophet Unarmed*, p. 32.

16 Lenin, 'Political Report of the Central Committee', *Selected Works*, Vol. 3, p. 633.

17 E.H. Carr, *The Bolshevik Revolution*, Vol. 1, p. 235.

18 M. Weber, *The Theory of Social and Economic Organization*, p. 339, for example.

19 Lenin, 'Can the Bolsheviks Retain State Power?', *Selected Works*, Vol. 2, p. 366. This was not an isolated theme; see also *Selected Works*, Vol. 2, pp. 46 and 266.

20 Cited Richard B. Day, *Leon Trotsky and the Politics of Economic Isolation*, pp. 44-5.

21 See Lenin, 'Five Years of the Russian Revolution and the Prospects of the World Revolution', *Selected Works*, Vol. 3, p. 674.

22 Lenin, 'Regulatory Order on the Work of Deputies', cited Lenin and Trotsky, *Lenin's Fight Against Stalinism*(sic), pp. 70-1.

23 Trotsky, 'Comments on Lenin's Proposal Concerning the Work of Deputies', ibid., p. 79.

24 Ibid., p. 80.

25 See Franz Schurmann, *Ideology and Organization in Communist China*, p. 188.

26 Lenin, 'Better Fewer, But Better', *Selected Works*, Vol. 3, p. 726.

27 Cited Carr, *The Bolshevik Revolution*, Vol. 1, p. 229.

28 Cited Raya Dunayevskaya, *Marxism and Freedom*, p. 200.
29 Lenin, 'One Step Forward, Two Steps Back', *Selected Works*, Vol. 1, p. 398.
30 Carr, *The Bolshevik Revolution*, Vol. 2, p. 290.
31 Alec Nove, *An Economic History of the USSR*, p. 87.
32 See Carr, *The Bolshevik Revolution*, Vol. 2, p. 302. This position is based on the assumption that urban industry commands the economy in a predominantly agricultural country.
33 Nove, p. 95; see also Maurice Dobb, *Soviet Economic Development Since 1917*, p. 162.
34 Max Shachtman, 'Ten Years', in *Education for Socialists Bulletin, Towards a History of the Fourth International*, Part V, p. 8.
35 Lenin, *The State and Revolution, Selected Works*, Vol. 2, p. 318. Nikolai Bukharin and Evgenii Preobrazhensky, *The ABC of Communism*, p. 240.
36 Trotsky defined 'culture' very broadly; see *Leon Trotsky on Literature and Art*, p. 54.
37 Lenin, 'Better Fewer, But Better', p. 721.
38 Trotsky, *The Real Situation in Russia*, p. 112.
39 R.V. Daniels, *The Nature of Communism*, p. 277.
40 Daniels, *The Conscience of the Revolution*, p. 238; see also Leonard Schapiro, *The Communist Party of the Soviet Union*, p. 314.
41 N. Krupskaya, 'The Lessons of October', J.T. Murphy (ed.), *The Errors of Trotskyism*.
42 Deutscher, *The Prophet Unarmed*, pp. 249–50.
43 See *Leon Trotsky on Britain*, pp. 253 and 273.
44 Cited Daniels, *The Conscience of the Revolution*, p. 278.
45 Cited E.H. Carr and R.W. Davies, *Foundations of a Planned Economy*, Vol. 1, p. 300.
46 Cited Deutscher, *The Prophet Armed*, p. 90.
47 Cited Daniels, *The Conscience of the Revolution*, p. 150.
48 Deutscher, *The Prophet Unarmed*, p. 115.
49 Howe, p. 84.
50 Trotsky, *Portraits*, p. 179.
51 Trotsky, *Problems of Everyday Life*, p. 75.
52 Ibid., p. 104.
53 Ibid., p. 109.
54 Ibid., p. 111.

3. THE TRIAL

1 Deutscher, *The Prophet Outcast*, p. 89.
2 Trotsky, *The Third International After Lenin*, p. 61.
3 Trotsky, '1929 Introduction', *The Permanent Revolution*, p. 133.
4 Day, p. 105.
5 Cited Deutscher, *The Prophet Outcast*, p. 143.
6 Trotsky, *The Struggle Against Fascism in Germany*, pp. 379–80.
7 Ibid., p. 390.

4. BOLSHEVISM BETRAYED

1 See O. Kuusinen (ed.), *Fundamentals of Marxism-Leninism*, p. 561.
2 Knei-Paz, p. 385.
3 Richard Day's work relies upon the idea that during the war communism period Trotsky 'emerged as the central theorist of economic isolation' (p. 5), only reversing his view in the mid-1920s.
4 Marx and Engels, *Selected Works*, Vol. 3, p. 328.
5 Lenin, *Collected Works*, Vol. 25, p. 180.
6 Lenin, *The State and Revolution*, p. 272.
7 Marx, 'Critique of the Gotha Programme', *Selected Works*, Vol. 3, p. 26.
8 Yet cf. Trotsky, *Terrorism and Communism*, pp. 169–70: 'the road to Socialism lies through a period of the highest possible intensification of the principle of the State'.
9 Marx, 'Critique of the Gotha Programme', p. 19.
10 Lenin, *The State and Revolution*, p. 310.
11 Ibid.
12 John Plamenatz, 'Deviations from Marxism', *The Political Quarterly*, Vol. 21, No. 1, 1950, p. 54.
13 Trotsky, *Portraits*, p. 66.
14 Trotsky, *Stalinism and Bolshevism*, p. 10.
15 T.H. Rigby, *Communist Party Membership in the USSR, 1917–67*, Chapter 3, especially p. 131.
16 Ivan Szelenyi, 'The Position of the Intelligentsia in the Class Structure of State Socialist Societies', unpublished paper, Flinders University, 1977, pp. 19–20.
17 See Lenin, 'Letter to the Congress', *Selected Works*, Vol. 3, pp. 685–9.

18 Trotsky, *Stalin*, Vol. 2, p. 138. See also R.H. McNeal, 'Trotsky's Interpretation of Stalin', *Canadian Slavonic Papers*, Vol. 5, 1961, pp. 87–97.

19 Knei-Paz, p. 529.

20 Trotsky, *Portraits*, p. 183.

21 Trotsky, *The Third International After Lenin*, p. 125.

22 Ibid., pp. 304–5.

23 On its earliest uses, see Deutscher, *The Prophet Unarmed*, pp. 244–5. On Trotsky's changing assessments of 'Thermidor', see Siegfried Bahne, 'Trotsky on Stalin's Russia', *Survey*, 41, April 1962, pp. 27–42.

24 Winston Churchill, 'Leon Trotsky *alias* Bronstein', *Great Contemporaries*, p. 163.

25 Karl Kautsky, *The Labour Revolution*, p. 61.

26 See Max Shachtman, *The Bureaucratic Revolution*, Chapter 5.

27 Marx and Engels, *The Communist Manifesto, Selected Works*, Vol. 1, p. 126.

28 Lenin, *The State and Revolution*, p. 302.

29 See Lenin, 'Economics and Politics in the Era of the Dictatorship of the Proletariat', *Selected Works*, Vol. 3, p. 232.

30 K. Mavrakis, *On Trotskyism*, p. 77.

31 See Lenin, 'Re the Monopoly of Foreign Trade', *Selected Works*, Vol. 3, pp. 659–65.

32 In 1843, Marx wrote that 'The bureaucracy has the state... in its possession, as its *private property*', *Contribution to the Critique of Hegel's Philosophy of Law, Collected Works*, Vol. 3, p. 47.

33 See A.A. Berle and G.C. Means, *The Modern Corporation and Private Property*.

34 Milovan Djilas, however, has argued that the Soviet bureaucracy enjoys 'collective ownership' of the means of production, *The New Class*, p. 53.

35 A. Nove, 'The Class Nature of the Soviet Union Revisited', *Soviet Studies*, Vol. 35, No. 3, July 1983, p. 310.

36 See David Lane, *The Socialist Industrial State*, p. 185.

37 Marx, '1859 Preface', *A Contribution to the Critique of Political Economy, Selected Works*, Vol. 1, p. 503.

38 Ibid.

39 Trotsky, *The Transitional Program for Socialist Revolution*, p. 102.

5. BOLSHEVISM REAFFIRMED

1 Khrushchev raised this event in his 'Secret Speech' to the Twentieth Congress of the CPSU in 1956. See his 'Twentieth Congress Report', in G. Healey et al, *The Moscow Trials: An Anthology*, pp. 21-2.
2 Cited Deutscher, *The Prophet Outcast*, p. 335.
3 See, however, Peter Deli, 'The *Manchester Guardian* and the Soviet Purges 1936-38', *Survey*, Vol. 28, No. 1, 1984, pp. 119-65, for an account of a newspaper whose editorialists and Moscow correspondent were not deceived, and which opened its letters columns to diverse views on the subject of the purge trials and their significance.
4 See Deutscher, *The Prophet Outcast*, p. 336, and Victor Serge and Natalya Sedov, *The Life and Death of Leon Trotsky*, p. 208.
5 Trotsky, 'I Stake My Life!', *Leon Trotsky Speaks*, p. 277.
6 See J. Dewey, *Not Guilty: Report of the Commission of Inquiry*.
7 See R.C. Tucker, *The Soviet Political Mind*, Chapter 3, and Robert Conquest, *The Great Terror*.
8 Trotsky, *Diary in Exile*, pp. 46-7.
9 See Deutscher, *The Prophet Outcast*, p. 124.
10 M.B., 'Trotskyists at Vorkuta', G. Saunders (ed.), *Samizdat*, p. 206.
11 See Deutscher, *The Prophet Outcast*, pp. 422-9.
12 Trotsky responded with 'Not a Workers' and Not a Bourgeois State?', *Writings of Leon Trotsky, 1937-38*, p. 60.
13 Cited Hansen and Warde, p. ix.
14 In 1941, in *The Managerial Revolution*, Burnham argued that the USSR was one example of an entirely new form of society: 'managerial society'.
15 For more information on the mysterious Bruno R, see Daniel Bell, 'The Strange Tale of Bruno R', *The New Leader*, 28 September 1959, pp. 19-20. As Bell points out, the 'new class' theories current during the 1930s (and taken up later by Djilas, among others), may be traced to the work of the Polish socialist Jan Waclaw Machajski. See also Marian Sawer, 'Theories of the New Class from Bakunin to Kuron and Modzelewski', in Sawer (ed.), *Socialism and the New Class*, pp. 6-9.
16 John G. Wright, 'Trotsky's Struggle for the Fourth International', *Leon Trotsky: The Man and His Work*, p. 69.
17 See W. Reisner (ed.), *Documents of the Fourth International*, pp. 291-4.
18 See James P. Cannon, *The Struggle for a Proletarian Party*, p. 100.
19 Ibid., p. 86.
20 Trotsky, *Leon Trotsky Speaks*, p. 298.

6. CONCLUSION

1 Howe, p. 144. Like most moralists, however, Trotsky seemed to sense his impotence. While the major metaphors of Marx evoke the idea of new life ('pregnant', 'womb', 'birth'), Trotsky's are devoted to death and decay ('degeneration', 'abcess', 'gangrene', 'corpse').

2 *The Case of Leon Trotsky*, p. 361.

BIBLIOGRAPHY OF WORKS CITED

BAHNE, S., 'Trotsky on Stalin's Russia', *Survey*, No. 41, April 1962, pp. 27–42.

BELL, D., 'The Strange Tale of Bruno R', *The New Leader*, Vol. 42, No. 36, 28 September 1959, pp. 19–20.

BERLE, A.A. and MEANS, G.C., *The Modern Corporation and Private Property*, Harcourt, Brace and World, NY, 1967.

BUKHARIN, N. and PREOBRAZHENSKY, E., *The ABC of Communism*, edited E.H. Carr, Penguin, Harmondsworth, 1970.

BURNHAM, J., *The Managerial Revolution*, Penguin, Harmondsworth 1962.

CANNON, J.P., *The Struggle for a Proletarian Party*, Pathfinder, NY, 1972.

CARR, E.H., *The Bolshevik Revolution*, Vols. 1 and 2, Penguin, Harmondsworth, 1973 and 1972.

CARR, E.H., *The Interregnum 1923-24*, Penguin, Harmondsworth, 1969.

CARR, E.H. and DAVIES, R.W., *Foundations of a Planned Economy, 1926-1929*, Vol. 1, Penguin, Harmondsworth, 1974.

CHURCHILL, W., *Great Contemporaries*, Fontana, London, 1959.

CONQUEST, R., *The Great Terror: Stalin's Purge of the Thirties*, Penguin, Harmondsworth, 1974.

DANIELS, R.V., *The Conscience of the Revolution: Communist Opposition in Soviet Russia*, Simon and Schuster, NY, 1969.

DANIELS, R.V., *The Nature of Communism*, Vintage, NY, 1962.

DAY, R.B., *Leon Trotsky and the Politics of Economic Isolation*, Cambridge University Press, Cambridge, 1973.

DELI, P., 'The *Manchester Guardian* and the Soviet Purges 1936-38', *Survey*, Vol. 28, No. 1, 1984, pp. 119–65.

DEUTSCHER, I., *The Prophet Armed, Trotsky 1879-1921*, Oxford University Press, London, 1970.

DEUTSCHER, I., *The Prophet Unarmed, Trotsky 1921-1929*, Vintage, NY, 1959.

DEUTSCHER, I., *The Prophet Outcast, Trotsky 1929-1940*, Vintage, NY, 1963.

DEWEY, J., *Not Guilty: Report of the Commission of Inquiry into the Charges made against Leon Trotsky in the Moscow Trials*, Monad, NY, 1972.

DJILAS, M., *The New Class*, Unwin, London, 1966.

DOBB, M., *Soviet Economic Development Since 1917*, Routledge and Kegan Paul, London, 1966.

DUNAYEVSKAYA, R., *Marxism and Freedom*, Pluto, London, 1975.

EASTMAN, M., *Since Lenin Died*, Hyperion, Connecticut, 1972.

GETZLER, I., *Kronstadt 1917-1921. The Fate of a Soviet Democracy*, Cambridge University Press, Cambridge, 1983.

HAMPSON, N., *The Life and Opinions of Maximilien Robespierre*, Duckworth, London, 1974.

HANSEN, J. (et al), *Leon Trotsky: The Man and His Work*, Merit, NY, 1969.

HEALEY. G. (et al), *The Moscow Trials: An Anthology*, New Park, London, 1967.

KAUTSKY, K., *The Labour Revolution*, translated H.J. Stenning, Allen and Unwin, 1925.

KNEI-PAZ, B., *The Social and Political Thought of Leon Trotsky*, Oxford University Press, Oxford, 1978.

KUUSINEN, O.V. (ed.), *Fundamentals of Marxism-Leninism*, FLPH, Moscow, 1963.

LANE, D., *The Socialist Industrial State*, Allen and Unwin, London, 1976.

LENIN, V.I., *Selected Works* (in three volumes), Progress, Moscow, 1976.

LENIN, V.I., *Collected Works*, Vols. 25-27, Progress, Moscow, 1977.

LOVELL, D.W., *From Marx to Lenin. An Evaluation of Marx's Responsibility for Soviet Authoritarianism*, Cambridge University Press, Cambridge, 1984.

McNEAL, R.H., 'Trotsky's Interpretation of Stalin', *Canadian Slavonic Papers*, Vol. 5, 1961, pp. 87-97.

MARX, K. and ENGELS, F., *Collected Works*, Vol. 3, Lawrence and Wishart, London and Progress, Moscow, 1975.

MARX, K. and ENGELS, F., *Selected Works* (in three volumes), Progress, Moscow, 1975.

MAVRAKIS, K., *On Trotskyism*, Routledge and Kegan Paul, London, 1976.

MURPHY, J.T. (ed.), *The Errors of Trotskyism*, Communist Party of Great Britain, London, 1925.

NOVE, A., *An Economic History of the USSR*, Penguin, Harmondsworth, 1972.

NOVE, A., 'The Class Nature of the Soviet Union Revisited', *Soviet Studies*, Vol. 35, No. 3, July 1983, pp. 298-312.

ORWELL, G., *The Collected Essays, Journalism and Letters of George*

Orwell, Vol. 4, edited S. Orwell and I. Angus, Penguin, Harmondsworth, 1970.

PLAMENATZ, J., *German Marxism and Russian Communism*, Longmans, London, 1965.

PLAMENATZ, J., 'Deviations from Marxism', *The Political Quarterly*, Vol. 21, No. 1, 1950, pp. 40–55.

REISNER, W. (ed.), *Documents of the Fourth International (1933-40)*, Pathfinder, NY, 1973.

RIGBY, T.H., *Communist Party Membership in the USSR, 1917-1967*, Princeton University Press, NJ, 1968.

SAUNDERS, G. (ed.), *Samizdat: Voices of the Soviet Opposition*, Monad, NY, 1974.

SAWER, M. (ed.), *Socialism and the New Class: Towards the Analysis of Structural Inequality Within Socialist Societies*, APSA Monograph, No. 19, 1978.

SCHAPIRO, L., *The Communist Party of the Soviet Union*, Eyre and Spottiswoode, London, 1970.

SCHURMANN, F., *Ideology and Organization in Communist China*, University of California Press, Berkley, 1973.

SEGAL, R., *The Tragedy of Leon Trotsky*, Hutchinson, London, 1977.

SERGE, V. and SEDOV, N., *The Life and Death of Leon Trotsky*, translated A.J. Pomerans, Basic Books, NY, 1975.

SHACHTMAN, M., *The Bureaucratic Revolution*, Donald Press, NY, 1962.

SHACHTMAN, M., 'Ten Years', *Towards a History of the Fourth International*, Part V, *Education for Socialists Bulletin*.

SZELENYI, I., 'The Position of the Intelligentsia in the Class Structure of State Socialist Societies', unpublished paper, Flinders University of South Australia, March 1977.

TROTSKY, L., *The Challenge of the Left Opposition (1923-25)*, edited N. Allen, Pathfinder, NY, 1975.

TROTSKY, L., *Their Morals and Ours. Marxist versus liberal views on morality*, edited G. Novack, Pathfinder, NY,1972.

TROTSKY, L., *Portraits, Political and Personal*, edited G. Breitman and G. Saunders, Pathfinder, NY, 1977.

TROTSKY, L., *The Real Situation in Russia*, translated M. Eastman, Allen and Unwin, London, n.d.

TROTSKY, L., *The Third International After Lenin*, Pathfinder, NY, 1970.

TROTSKY, L., *My Life*, Pathfinder, NY, 1970.

TROTSKY, L., *Diary in Exile*, translated E. Zarudnaya, Harvard University Press, Massachusetts, 1958.

TROTSKY, L., *The Permanent Revolution and Results and Prospects*, Pathfinder, NY, 1972.

TROTSKY, L., *The Struggle Against Fascism in Germany*, Penguin, Harmondsworth, 1975.

TROTSKY, L., *The Revolution Betrayed*, translated M. Eastman, Pathfinder, NY, 1970.

TROTSKY, L., *Writings of Leon Trotsky (1929-40)* (in twelve volumes), Pathfinder, NY, 1969-77.

TROTSKY, L., *The Transitional Program for Socialist Revolution*, Pathfinder, NY, 1973.

TROTSKY, L., *Stalinism and Bolshevism*, SYA pamphlet, Sydney, n.d.

TROTSKY, L., *Leon Trotsky on Literature and Art*, edited P.N. Siegel, Pathfinder, NY, 1970.

TROTSKY, L., *The Case of Leon Trotsky*, Merit, NY, 1969.

TROTSKY, L., *Problems of Everyday Life*, Monad, NY, 1973.

TROTSKY, L., *Leon Trotsky on Britain*, Monad, NY, 1973.

TROTSKY, L., *Stalin: An Appraisal of the Man and his Influence*, two volumes, Panther, London, 1969.

TROTSKY, L., *In Defense of Marxism*, Pathfinder, NY, 1970.

TROTSKY, L., *Leon Trotsky Speaks*, edited S. Lovell, Pathfinder, NY, 1972.

TROTSKY, L., *Terrorism and Communism, A Reply to Karl Kautsky*, University of Michigan Press, Ann Arbor, 1963.

TROTSKY, L. and LENIN, V.I., *Lenin's Struggle Against Stalinism*, edited R. Black, Pathfinder, NY, 1975.

TUCKER, R.C., *The Soviet Political Mind*, Allen and Unwin, London, 1972.

WEBER, M., *The Theory of Social and Economic Organization*, edited T. Parsons, Free Press, NY, 1964.

INDEX